Unlocking the Classroom Door

by

Jennifer León Hill

DORRANCE
PUBLISHING CO
EST. 1920
PITTSBURGH, PENNSYLVANIA 15238

Dorrance Publishing Co
585 Alpha Drive
Pittsburgh, PA 15238
Visit our website at www.dorrancebookstore.com

ISBN: 979-8-88729-212-0
eISBN: 979-8-88729-712-5

Dedication

Dedicated to the many students I've met along the way, who had an impact on my style of teaching and perception of children in general. There are so many others who know who they are, and I thank them profusely.

Introduction

I never expected to have some of the experiences I had when I embarked on a career in education. Every story you read in this book is completely factual with zero embellishments. This is not meant to be a biography but a compilation of my experiences as a contracted teacher, business owner, and substitute teacher. It will jump around in some areas, but I will make every effort to maintain a timeline without really giving dates, places, or names. I am brutally honest, and although it may seem offensive, you will appreciate it as you continue to read. This compilation is a "fly on the wall" look into the realities of being a teacher from 1995–2017.

Teachers' Human Behavior: Teachers Are Not Angels

A common perception of teachers is that they are open, warm, friendly, loving, and accepting humans whose only interest in this world is to help everyone become successful. I have been a classroom teacher and a substitute teacher, and I have spoken to numerous education professionals including paraprofessionals, cafeteria staff, office staff, and crossing guards. Education personnel are all humans who have feelings and are no more special than many other humans. They form cliques, they shut people out of parties, they gossip about their students and each other, they curse and hate, and they get very angry when they are mistreated. They are not gods or heroes but regular people doing a job at their place of business. They can be sweet to your face and mean behind your back. They can spread terrible lies about you or ignore you even though they've met you many times. Some walk so tall and proud that the average person or lowly substitute cannot come close to them. However you feel about teachers/education professionals, always remember they are humans and you can talk to them. They are around your children every day, and although we must respect them and be polite, you can be heard. Treat them as you would like to be treated, and things will go very well. Treat them with demands and rude, entitled behavior, and you will not get a good education for your child. You may not want to believe it, but they do take it out on your children when you treat them with disrespect.

I had been a substitute teacher in the same three or four schools for six years. I saw students at the junior high level and then a few years later at the high school. They always remember me and tell me where I previously subbed for them. I just love to hear this, and it makes my day. I enjoy walking into any given classroom, at any of these schools and hear, "Yes, it's Mrs. Hill! My favorite sub!" I recently had a few students in an eighth-grade class say, "Remember me? You subbed in my sixth-grade class!"

The flip side is that after subbing as many years in the same three to four schools, primarily grades eight to twelve, the teachers still treat me like a stranger. I have had personal conversations with many of these teachers as well as teachers I've never subbed for, over the years. I've attended assemblies with them or even helped at the school fair because I was subbing that day as it was the last period of my subbing day. I've sat with them in the lunchroom many times and given my phone and sub number out over and over again. I never get phone calls or texts to sub, and when I see those same teachers on campus, they treat me as though they have never seen me before.

Why would they act like that? I refer to my first sentence in this section. Being a substitute is not only low pay, no benefits, little to no breaks, and being treated to the students' worst behavior but also being snubbed by teachers on campus. They say there is a substitute shortage, so why treat them so poorly?

Why I Became a Teacher

As a young girl in Arizona, I had big dreams to be a mother and teacher. Life started simply enough with a mommy, a daddy, and smaller siblings. Although many details are irrelevant, I'll keep it simple to help the reader understand how I came to the point of writing this particular book.

Like many head-in-the-clouds girls in the 1970s, I wanted to be a bride, a mother, and a teacher. I was not sure in what order it would occur, but that all are achieved in time. School went by quickly with little incident, and by the time I got to high school, I was small, shy, and losing my drive. I was in the marching band and found my passion in music. I aspired to be a band teacher and really focused on making music my life. I didn't have boyfriends in high school, as I didn't care about my appearance much. I was so quiet but had big thoughts and dreams. Marching band and my two or three friends were everything to me. Life became more difficult, as I hated academics but knew I had to keep it together for music. I needed to graduate and go on to college where I could fulfill my dreams.

By the time I went to college, I had to work many jobs so I could live away from my parents and pay for school. I did well in my one year at community college, but when I got to

Arizona State University (ASU), I was struggling and allowing other things in life to derail me. After flunking out of ASU (and the music program), getting married, having children at the age of twenty-one, and working at a golf course selling beers and sandwiches, I met my inspiration to go back to college.

While working as a beer cart girl, I had many shifts with a woman simply nicknamed "Red." She and I would work together frequently, since I was young and inexperienced, and she was a seasoned veteran at the job. I became quite good at interacting with the golfers and developed a rapport with many regulars and course supervisors. On the anniversary of my second year at the job, Red approached me with kind words of advice and encouragement to make this my career. Mind you, Red had been a beverage cart girl on golf courses for twenty years, and her leathered skin, smoke-induced raspy voice, and dyed long red hair showed her age. As I looked into her earnest but exhausted eyes, listening to her kind words saying to me, "Jennifer, you have all of the characteristics and drive of becoming a career-long, beverage cart girl," I internally cringed and thought to myself, *I must do whatever I have to do to find a better career choice.* Sometimes in life we meet people who influence us in different ways, either negatively or positively. Little did she know, she was my inspiration for pursuing a career in teaching, which required me to finish my college degree.

Moving forward on my timeline, I graduated high school in 1988 and graduated college in 1997, as a certified elementary school teacher. I knew teaching would be the right profession because I could be home with my children on weekends, holidays, and summers. The downside to being a teacher is that you can rarely help in your child's classroom, attend daytime parent/teacher conferences, field day, in-school fairs or carnivals, or go on fieldtrips with them. Of course, one can always take days off, but realistically, how many days can a teacher take off in a given school year?

1997–1999 Elementary School (K–6)

I began my teaching career as a fifth-grade general studies teacher. This school was in an extremely poor, migrant worker neighborhood called The Square, in Phoenix, Arizona. Several thousand people lived within one square mile of the school. At age twenty-seven, I finally finished college and the teaching program, and was ready to embark on this new challenge. I had just given birth to my second son and felt life had prepared me to teach children. I never expected that dealing with the adults would be the largest challenge I would face. The older, more experienced teachers treated me as though I was a young, inexperienced idiot and never failed to tell me so. I never had a voice in the two years I was at this school, and when I tried to contribute my opinions or ideas, they were shot down or called ridiculous. A little-known fact I will reveal over and over in this book is: teachers are the most judgmental, petty, jealous, and mean people in the workforce.

As a fifth-grade teacher, I assigned my students classwork, and when it wasn't completed in class, it was homework. I had high expectations of the students and required them to be thoughtful and rigorous in their quality of work. I spent every minute of every class day talking to the students, working with them individually, and never resting. I exhausted myself but knew the students were thriving. There were a few who complained that none of the other classes had so much work, but they always worked hard for me.

Fellow fifth-grade, older teachers would corner me in the lunch room to chastise me. Often, I would be sitting at a table eating my lunch, and they would loom over me, leaning on the table in intimidation. They said I was expecting too much from our students. They told me I was not allowed to assign homework because the students' home lives were tough enough already. They said these kids have siblings to care for or parents who are abusive, drug addicted, or often not home at all. While I agreed these particular students had circumstances often perceived to not be experienced by other, more affluent families, they still deserved to learn like other students. Parents at our school did not often attend parent-teacher conferences, and I overheard some of the students talk about their home lives. I had my eyes open but wanted the students to have access to a high level of education as well.

My responses to these looming teachers were that to lower expectations of challenging schoolwork or never assigning homework was really putting our students at various disadvantages in life. Many students thought school should always be easy, and it created a culture of laziness. These fellow teachers warned me to never assign projects or homework in fifth grade. If this is how I must comply, fine, so I decided that there would not be assigned homework, but when in class, I still expected every minute to be consumed with learning and trying. Again, I was reprimanded by the elders for even pushing them hard in class. It began to be tiresome to go to the lunchroom, so I sequestered myself in my room, never making friends or having adult interaction.

Invariably, some of the kids would have homework for one reason or another, and these ladies would find out. Knowing I was hiding in my room, they would barge in, stand over me, and shout. These teachers would tell me that they are Jewish and talked about how their religion teaches compassion and I clearly didn't have any. Although religion in comparison to teaching never crossed my mind, these ladies reminded me about their religion, every chance they had. Mind you, this was being yelled at me while I was sitting at my desk, and they would lean in closer to my face. I had heard the first year as a teacher was tough but never imagined this was the reason. This was too much. One cannot imagine what their reasoning was for barraging me with insults and reprimands, but I came to find out their self-ascribed motto was, No Hard Work. How dare I come into their school, in their grade, and have expectations of these poor, innocent, put upon children?! According to these teachers, school is an escape for these kids, and we needed to make sure it isn't stressful in any way. We must provide a safe haven with no stress or worries. They come to school hungry and dirty, and we must coddle and feed them as if they were ours.

I have children of my own and I am a teacher. I am educated and trained to be a teacher, not a social worker. Boy, would I learn throughout my career how wrong I was about that previous sentence.

I did not sit silently through the attacks and spoke loudly in response to these overweight, overbearing, nasty-minded, bleeding-heart teachers. I told them I will continue on my path to educating these students. I also told them they do not need to be concerned with what I do behind my classroom door and they can kindly leave me to my lunch. The funny part was the assignment we were working on in class was memorizing the names of the presidents of the United States, in order. We practiced as a class and in pairs, several times a day, and although the kids were concerned about their abilities, they were getting really good. I was orally testing them later in the week. It's a test, and of course there's a bit of stress, which is completely normal. I was proud of them, and they were learning.

My stance on my colleagues' opinions did not make them happy, but I forged on. As frustrated as they were with me, most of my students got high marks on the oral test, and those who didn't practiced with me for a few more days and re-tested very well. My students were very proud of themselves and bragged to the other students in other classes. None of the other fifth-grade students could recite the presidents' names in order! Could they even name a few of them? No!

It makes me wonder why these teachers were so concerned with what I was doing with my students. The kids loved them, as they were warm and cuddly with love and smiles all the time. Go be a pre-school teacher, then. If they weren't jealous of me, why get on my case so much? Did I make them look bad? Who will ever know, but they certainly made me feel awful. I went home and cried a lot those two years, but I kept my resolve firm. My students completed in-class writing assignments while I played classical music, sang math songs, and I read to them every day, which they loved. They also wrote essays, memorized facts, and had timed math quizzes often. They progressed and learned, and that was what I was hired to do.

The harassment I endured did not only come from other teachers but from the principal as well. He was happy with my teaching but unhappy I could not attend every staff meeting or come to school extra early every day. Every teaching contract in our district dictates our workday hours as first class bell to after the last class leaves, so I was neither required to be early nor could do it. I had a husband who worked nights and couldn't help with our two small children, and part way through the first year, I became pregnant with my third son. I had to get up, get the boys and myself ready, drop them off at my mother's house twenty minutes away, and get myself to school before the bell at 8:30 a.m. I spoke to the principal and made arrangements to get all of the meeting information from other teachers. I worked many, many nights to make sure my grading and grades were up to date, but I just couldn't be early to work. Unfortunately, the administrators and others in my school refused to understand or remember the constant conversations regarding this issue. I had my back up against the wall at this point.

After two years of consistent harassment and much discussion with the principal, I decided to take a one-year leave of absence. The prospect of continuing as a teacher under these conditions seemed overwhelming, and I was already burnt out. Those women beat me emotionally, the principal reprimanded me often for not being early to school or absent from staff meetings, and the teacher's union took my money, time, and desire.

Sadly, this happens to so many teachers just starting out, no matter one's age or other life experiences. Teaching tends to be an elitist profession, and once certified and employed, the tendency is to condescend each other, and act superior. Between the low pay, lack of respect, and understanding for those who have families or life situations, it is a daunting task to be a teacher. At the same time, parents want you to be their child's friend, mentor, confidant, feed them, and make them feel good about life. Teachers are expected to be there before and after school for staff meetings, department meetings, grade-level meetings, parent meetings, and Individual Education Plan (IEP) meetings. They are expected to spend their personal break/prep and lunch period making copies, making parent phone calls, returning emails, planning for class, grading papers, cleaning the classroom, and even asked to fill in as a sub when there is not a sub to fill an absence. There is not one minute of any day where we can actually have time to relax or regroup or even shove a sandwich down our throats.

By the time each day is over, a teacher is emotionally and physically drained. They drag a giant bag of papers to their car so they can grade them while eating dinner or after putting their own children to bed. As well, teachers must remember to stop at the store for groceries, get their own children to various events and then home. Coming home means cleaning, dinner, helping their children with their homework, discipline, and bedtime. At that time a teacher can now sit at the table and grade a few papers before falling into bed. Do we ever wonder why teachers are usually overweight, unhealthy, tired looking, out of shape, unkempt, and generally short of temper? Many teachers decompress by drinking with their friends and overeating. But we do it because we love children and it is a calling, right? Sure!

Repeatedly I have been told, "Well, at least you have a job and benefits." Yes, they are right. I am grateful to be employed and putting my college education to work. However, I would probably make more money and have far less stress if I worked at a fast-food restaurant or chain department store. "You have weekends, summers, and holidays off. Come on, we wish we had that!" Yes, we do love that, but our weekends and holidays are spent playing catch up on grading, planning, housework, projects, and making up for neglecting our families during the week. Summer means desperately looking for free things to do to keep our children occupied or possibly pursuing a higher-learning degree. Many teachers seek summer jobs to supplement their pay even though they can obtain exclusive mortgage and student loan deferrals, simply because they are teachers.

Summer is also spent getting ready for the upcoming school year or taking classes so we can keep our teaching certificate. If we want a pay raise, we have to keep taking classes. At some point in the summer, every teacher tells themselves, "I can do this! I love my job! I love the kids! I'm going to have better control over the students! I'm going to have a whole new way for my grading system and get better at time management! I'm going to get to the gym a few times a week! I'm going to be an inspiration to all with my fresh ideas! I can do this!"

Fools, all of us!

Moving On

There came a time when I had to make a major decision about the trajectory of my life. In the year 1999, I had been teaching fifth grade full time, caring for my home, three very young sons, and in an extremely trying marriage. Crossroads in life became so difficult that I knew something had to give. I decided to take a one-year leave of absence from my job, in an effort to keep the family together. After about six months, a decision had to be made about me returning to the classroom, as the district was trying to offer me a contract for the upcoming school year. Time had really flown! A friend and fellow teacher and I decided there had to be a way to stay home indefinitely with our babies, and still bring in money for the family.

My friend and I started a tutoring company and began the arduous journey of advertising and gaining business, where we hired professional, licensed, and fingerprinted teachers to do one-on-one tutoring, in people's homes. The families paid us a fee, and we paid the teachers a portion of that fee. We traveled from school to school in several different districts and talked to many office staff and people. The two of us did all of the tutoring jobs for the first few months, to save money. We knew we needed to recruit teachers to work for us and put flyers everywhere. We had legal contracts and even liability insurance policies. It was not easy but became mildly successful after only one year. Into year two, we were still not making much money, but I wanted to continue to see it through. My friend felt differently and needed steady income with benefits, so I bought her portion of the business and continued to run it by myself. Needless to say, a one-year leave of absence became a resignation from teaching all together. Reality really began to set in.

Reflection

There are things about teaching which the public may not know. For example, if a certified teacher does not continue schooling or is not currently in the classroom teaching under contract, you lose your certificate and all you have worked so hard for. Many think being a teacher is simply "get your degree and certificate and teach with summer, weekends. and vacations off." This is not true. Teachers must continue to earn college credits (at their own expense), attend seminars in their spare time (at their own expense), or face losing their certificate of teaching. As well, we must attend workshops during the school year, in our private time if we wish to get any raises. To add to the fun, oftentimes the school district or the state Department of Education will sit in a big room and decide teachers need even more training in a particular area and require hours and hours of training on our own time. One of those mandates was to have thirty-six hours of training to be English as a Second Language (ESL) or English Language Learners (ELL) certified. Wouldn't a teacher love to spend more time doing research for your child? We love coming up with inventive lessons or strategies for teaching more effectively or grading papers your child completed instead of spending hours in seminars learning how to teach a student who does not know the English language. Funny how people think contracts and raises are automatically bestowed upon teachers every year! LOL! I wonder if the average fast-food worker who wants a higher wage would be okay with attending college classes, workshops, and seminars at their own expense, to get their "living wage" raise? Probably not. As such, teaching is not actually bell to bell but starts in the early morning and goes on into nights and weekends.

Continuing On

I was now faced with losing my teaching certificate due to non-use. I had to choose between my burgeoning tutoring business and continuing my education to retain the teaching certificate I attended college to earn. I chose to go back to school and earn my master's degree in Educational Leadership. Several years later, after student loan debt, three young sons, and a new master's degree, I decided to turn in my business owner's hat and jump back into the realm of teaching.

The Return

Returning to education in 2004, I was thoroughly amused to be accepted as a part-time seventh-grade Spanish teacher. I was not certified as an intermediate Spanish teacher, but no one cared. My certification was in elementary education only. I did have a life-long family background in the Spanish language as I am half-Mexican, and most family gatherings were spoken in a great deal of Spanish. I felt I was qualified, right?! Their current teacher took a leave of absence in October, and they needed a warm body to fill the position.

As I stepped into the role of Spanish teacher, I realized there were no textbooks and no real, defined curriculum. I immediately went out and bought a few posters and one book I could copy from. The teacher had locked up the cabinets in the classroom and would not give me access. She went on an emergency leave to care for her mother and knew she would be returning. Friendly. Of course, I never met her personally, as she left a week before I took the position.

I had a blast with these kids, teaching them basics and celebrating Mexican holidays with mini fiestas and such. The principal was very supportive, and it was a no-stress position. As the year progressed, another part-time teacher went on maternity leave and I took on her Literature classes, finishing out the year. My pay was calculated at a ninety percent contract, so it wasn't bad for a first time back, after thinking I wasn't going to work at all but needing a paycheck.

There was a situation which occurred during this partial year which left me questioning my return. Although my students were all seventh grade, some of them could not quite make sense out of the social system of a middle school. One of these students was a female who consistently asked to come to my room during lunch to hang out and get away from mean girls. She would talk to me as I worked on papers or planning, and I would listen with an interested and open face. I wanted her to feel she had someone who she could talk to and not be bullied or harassed by others, which she claimed was happening. Teachers are always taught to be on the lookout for depression or signs a student was not fitting in or upset. She just needed someone to talk to and I had the time.

After about four weeks of this situation, she admitted to me that I was her only friend and she cared for me. She always wanted to hug me, but I said no, it is not appropriate for an adult teacher to be physical with the students. I also alerted the counselors and administration. They reported back to me that she was depressed and thanked me for caring. Suddenly, one day I got an email to come see the principal after school. There was no context, so I headed there after the last bell. It was clearly a serious situation, and the room contained not only the principal but the counselor, and one other person I can only assume was a district lawyer. They quickly let me know that the student I was allowing to come to my room at lunch time had made a sexual harassment claim against me. I was shocked and begged them for more information! How can this be happening? They showed me a letter she claimed I wrote her, professing my love for her and the desire for her to be my girlfriend. I immediately told them this is not my handwriting but hers and asked if I could run to the classroom and grab a sample of her work to compare handwriting. They consented, and I was able to convince them I had no part in this, at all. I was allowed to go home after going into great detail about exactly what happened in the classroom at lunch and how I always kept my door open and stayed a distance away from her at all times. Apparently, she also claimed I was kissing her every day!

In the days to follow and making contact with her family and her again, the powers that be determined the girl was making false claims and pressed her for the truth. She finally relented and admitted she wanted attention from me, felt she was a lesbian, and thought it would be cool to have a teacher as a girlfriend. She ended up writing an apology letter to me, and they transferred her out of my class. It was a very traumatic experience, and I kept an even greater distance from my students, after that incident.

At the end of that year, they phased me out due to declining enrollment and I was on the job trail again. I knew I needed to work, and my youngest son was now in first grade. I had a friend who was the counselor at a middle school in Phoenix and they were looking for an English teacher. I was not certified (Highly Qualified) to be an English teacher, but it is my greatest strength, and I had quite a few college credits toward an English degree. I interviewed and got the job on the contingency that I would take the state test and become certified. If one has twenty-six college credits in a particular subject, one can automatically add an English highly qualified classification to their certification. However, I only had twenty-two credits, so I was required to take the Arizona Educator Proficiency Assessments (AEPA). After three attempts and ninety-five dollars times three (my personal cost), I passed! By December, I was a certified, highly qualified middle school English teacher.

As an aside from previous pages, I have never studied Spanish in school but can speak it, read, and write it. I attempted the AEPA Spanish test to be a Spanish teacher and failed just under the required pass percentage.

Middle School English

Teaching seventh- and eighth-grade English was the highlight of my career and when I really enjoyed my craft. Upon hearing of my chosen grade to teach, many people exclaim, "Yikes! Those kids are tough and mean." My reply is always, "I'm tough and mean as well, so it works for the both of us." There is a delicate balance between engaging a student and maintaining a strict discipline in the classroom. I always demanded respect from the kids, but that is only achieved if you not only demonstrate what respect looks like and respect them. Not all deserve respect but definitely deserve a chance or two.

One example of showing students respect is that one should always dress appropriately and maintain a level of respect for self by being clean and groomed. I cannot tell you how many teachers I have encountered who dress in sweatpants, slippers, T-shirts, cargo shorts, ponytails, no make-up, or tattered sneakers. We expect the kids to follow a dress code, but we have allowed our teachers to slough off the professional look in favor of comfort. It's easy for men who can put on a polo shirt and twill pants, but I have also witnessed many male teachers dress in tattered clothes, old T-shirts, faded jeans, sloppy grooming, and look practically homeless.

Some may say, "Kids do not know or care how we look, it is the content we deliver," but those people are wrong. Teachers are an example and a role model, and we must maintain an image. We are not their friends, we are not their parent, we are a guide in their lives, and if we don't take ourselves seriously, they will not take us seriously either. Most of us can remember when teachers were professionals, taught content, and were role models not "buddies." I remember when I thought my teacher lived at the school and was shocked to see her in the grocery store one day. Could this be a chicken-and-the-egg argument? Quite possibly.

I loved teaching middle school English but did not appreciate some of the horrible events which were brought down upon me throughout the five years I taught there. When a school has a domineering principal, it makes it difficult for the teachers to truly do their jobs and create a safe environment of learning. Eventually, teachers either leave the school in search of a better fit or they leave the profession all together, feeling burned out and defeated. Unfortunately, this was the case with me. I will not chronicle my entire five years here but give you a few vignettes so you can further understand some of the real troubling situations teachers go through. Love of the profession? Love of the children? Low pay? A lot of stress? Yes, yes, yes, yes.

In 2005, I earned a master's degree in Educational Leadership with an emphasis on becoming a principal or superintendent. I merely have to take the state test and I am qualified to take any of those jobs. The pay is excellent, but so is the responsibility. However, at that time I was not interested in being anything more than a teacher and loved the subject and age of my students. Our principal or vice principal felt a top-down approach was best when handling teachers and students. If you're not familiar with the top-down approach, I will simplify it for you, and you may relate with whatever job you may have now.

Discipline from Administration

A top-down, heavy-handed approach to managing people is never proper and makes people feel ineffective or devalued. An example of this is when a teacher or even several teachers choose to do an activity with their students which is not necessarily approved by the principal. During this school year, a teacher at our middle school had created a contest to make her kids more competitive and feel driven to do their homework (we were having a real problem with it at this school). She challenged the class that if they all turned in their homework for a month, she would publicly blend and eat whatever the students voted on. The students won the challenge, and at lunch one day, she brought out an extension cord, blender, and a bag of burgers. She placed everything on the top step of the library entrance where the entire student body could see her while they were having lunch outside. They wanted her to drink a hamburger, so she proceeded to blend and drink. The kids went wild with applause and laughter, and fun was had by all. When the principal found out what all the commotion was, he was unhappy. Instead of speaking to the teacher individually, he chose to send an email to the staff warning that if such activities are not approved by admin, they must not do it or be disciplined. He loved to send warning emails to the staff and constantly remind us that we could be "fired for this...fired for that..." This teacher was in her first year of teaching, she was super smart, and the kids loved her. It simply crushed her spirit, and she began down the arduous road to bitterness like so many teachers before her.

The same flawed approach to management is detrimental for students as well. Many students did not respect him for this very thing. We must always remember that children are wise and see things we may think they do not. Another example of a top-down approach was a pressing problem we were having at the middle school where some kids were bringing permanent markers to school and drawing on themselves and other student's bodies or clothing. Instead of dealing with the few offenders as we caught them, he chose to make a general announcement. During morning video announcements, he told the entire student body that if anyone is caught with a permanent marker in their possession or drawing on other people, they will be suspended and not go on the end-of-the-year field trip.

Most of the student body had no idea this was going on around the campus, and the next day, there were far more kids with permanent markers; it was out of control. This infuriated the principal even further and he made another, more threatening announcement, which the kids laughed at. If he had just talked to the teachers or made a friendly announcement without grave threats, it would have quietly gone away. We had the same issue with kids wearing hoodie sweatshirts and not putting their hoodie down when they got on campus. Previously, we would get the occasional kid try to put it up during class, but us teachers would modestly ask them to put it down so we could see their "beautiful faces." Unfortunately, the principal felt a top-down tact was best and made a dire warning announcement one morning, saying hoodies were banned. The result was more and more kids wore hoodies to school, and some innocent kids were very upset because they were simply cold. The top-down approach to leading isn't effective; punish the whole for the transgressions of a few. No thank you.

Middle School Parents

While teaching seventh-grade English, in the normal course of an average day, teachers will administer a vocabulary pop quiz. Every week they had spelling/vocabulary words along with a test, and sometimes I would give a quick ten-point pop quiz to keep them sharp. The kids all accepted it and understood in the grand scheme of their grades, this barely made a dent. However, one boy in one of my classes was unhappy about it. He came to me a few months into the school year, from another English class. I was told very little about him other than he just couldn't get along in this other teacher's class and the mother wanted him moved.

This boy filibustered with me to let him skip the pop quiz because he hasn't had a chance to do the homework or study yet. He said, "Wait, isn't the test Friday? It's only Thursday, so why do I have to do this?!" I informed him that, regardless, it is a good way to familiarize himself with the words. I also reminded him that I've given plenty of class time to work on the packet, so if he has not chosen to use his class time for that and hasn't even looked at the words, that is his fault, not mine. He stomped to his seat and pouted. Meanwhile, out of my 160-plus students, he was the only one to protest.

We self-grade pop quizzes, and I record those grades immediately as it is good for the kids to have immediate feedback on test prep. This particular student got a 7/10, which is a seventy percent, C-; not bad. He was upset but didn't say anything.

As an aside, earlier in this week I found out a student I had last year died, and her funeral was the next day. I was upset but tried not to let it affect my teaching. These kids didn't know her.

That evening after I got home, I saw an email from the pop quiz-protesting student's mother telling me how her son should have never had to take that quiz and how it made her son feel stupid and would I just excuse him from it all together, effectively wiping the grade clean. She went on to lecture me about why I shouldn't give pop quizzes and how I need to reevaluate how I teach. My initial reaction when I saw the email was to simply ignore it because it made me mad. As stated before, I have over 160 students throughout all my classes and not one protested or thought it was unfair. However, this one mother felt her son should get special treatment and be excused from a simple ten-point pop quiz and this was an injustice to the other 159 students. I wasn't going to excuse him, so I composed myself and wrote a reply email to her. I will admit, I probably should have left it alone, but my fingers flew on the keys, and I hit send before thinking twice. Needless to say, I was factual and curt, and she didn't like it one bit. I told her I wouldn't erase the grade and explained to her how her son hadn't even looked at his packet all week and that is his fault. I also told her that her son (here's the part I could have left out) isn't the only kid in the class and at least he's alive and doing fairly well.

The next day after starting my day with the students, the principal came to my room and wanted to talk to me in the back room. I told the kids to keep working, and he and I went just outside the classroom door. He told me that this mother was in his office and wanted me fired immediately if I didn't erase her son's grade on the pop quiz. What? Fired? I knew he couldn't fire me as there is a protocol and specific reasons to fire a teacher, and this isn't one of them. I told him I would not erase the grade and it isn't fair to the other 159 students who took the quiz and accepted their grades. I told him if he wanted to change it, that's on him, but I wouldn't do it. At no time did he ask me to tell him about the events of yesterday with this student and merely took the student and mother's word for it.

He stormed out of my room, and within an hour, an aide came to take over my classes. I was to gather all of my things and report to the office, in the middle of second period. I did so and encountered my union rep before going into his office. She said she would represent me and had been apprised of the situation. I asked her who apprised her because at no time was I asked to give my account. She said not to worry, she had my back. We walked in, and the principal started asking me a barrage of questions, none of them pertaining to this pop quiz incident but my personal character and ethics. I refused to answer, and my union rep sat mute. He then announced that I was being placed on administrative leave with pay based on insubordination, effective immediately. I did not get to say my side of the story at all, and my union rep still just sat there, looking confused.

At this particular year, my middle son was attending this same school, in the eighth grade. As I was driving home, he called me in a panic wanting to know if I'd been fired. I told him no, just suspended, and I will be there after school to pick him up. I also told him to stay quiet and not worry. As soon as I got home, I called the district office to find out what kind of recourse I had when being placed on admin leave. They immediately grew concerned and asked me a series of questions about my principal. Apparently, he told them I was very distraught and requested the time off. I informed them this was absolutely not true and gave them the whole story of how he pulled me out of class and so forth. They told me to report back to work first thing in the morning and they will handle the principal.

When I arrived at school the next morning, I went right for my room, got settled in, and ready for the day. The room was a mess, as the kids were being managed by random people throughout the day. For the kids, it was a wasted day, but for me, it was a learning experience about manipulation. The students started filing in, and the pop quiz-taking student came sauntering in, laughing and joking. As soon as he saw me, he truly did a triple-take, staring at me like I was a ghost. I waved and smiled and told him to take a seat.

It seems he told everyone that his mom got me fired and he was quite a grand hero all day, yesterday. Seeing me was a crushing blow to his ego, and other kids started laughing at him and pointing. I shut that down, right away, and sent the principal an email about exactly what happened. I told him he ought to talk to this kid and possibly his friends so he wouldn't get further bullied for being a liar. I also said that the principal himself brought this on by mishandling the situation. He never responded to my email, but I found out through other sources that he got disciplined by the district office officials for the way he handled me. I confronted my union rep and told her how she mishandled the situation and how she should seriously reconsider being a rep. As for the student, within a few days, he was transferred to another (his third that year) English class, where his mother continued to complain about things her son didn't want to do.

Teacher Evaluations

Every teacher is required to be formally observed by an administrator, usually two to four times a year. This is where the principal or assistant principal (AP) can get a glimpse into what the teacher's styles are, how the students behave, and what they are learning. My Formal Observation was this particular week, and it was business as usual for my class. As a veteran teacher, we know not to put in a special performance because that is not what a normal day looks like. First-year teachers feel like they have to do that, but it is not necessary; just teach. My class was in the middle of a lesson about a novel we were reading, so when the assistant principal walked into the room to observe, the entire class was silently reading.

I would like to mention that the assistant principal this year had been a Physical Education (PE) coach at this school for the past twenty years, and after getting certified, she landed the job as the assistant principal of this same school. She has never taught one day in a classroom, and neither has our current principal.

Additionally to this situation, the English department of this school meets every few weeks to plan together and make sure we are all on track as well as share ideas for lessons. We use a reading program called Accelerated Reader (AR) and are required to have the students read for a portion of the English class day. Some Social Studies teachers also offer silent reading time, as it is so beneficial for the student. Many do not take the time to read at home, and reading is fundamental to learning.

Previous to the day of my formal observation, I had submitted my lesson plans, and the AP knew we silently read for the beginning portion of the day, every day. She sat and waited and then observed as we did our warm-up grammar assignment, Daily Grams. The students take three minutes to complete a half-sheet of editing, spelling, grammar, and sentence combining. We, as a class, grade them together for the next three minutes and then move on. By the time we were done with our silent reading and warm-up, the AP got a call on her radio and had to leave. I continued about my lesson for the day, but she never returned. Later in the day, I got an email to meet in her office after school to discuss the observation. I replied asking her if she wanted a re-do and was welcome to come the next day, but she declined.

I really needed to get home to my children but sat waiting in her office for this meeting. When she finally came rushing into her office, she seemed harassed and flustered. She sat down and slapped an evaluation paper down on the table in from of me. I glanced at it quickly and noticed it said I was getting a poor score for wasting class time. She elaborated quickly by telling me that silent reading is not something we should be wasting class time on, and she sat and waited for me to teach them something. She also wrote that I did not teach anything this day and was requesting I go on probation for failure to complete the task of teaching. I was completely taken aback and expressed this to her immediately. I reiterated she was welcome to come back and observe again and she said of course she would, but I needed to sign this. I refused. No way would I accept this evaluation.

District policy says that if a teacher disagrees with an evaluation, they have the right to write an addendum to be added to their file. This does not erase the evaluation the administration writes up but simply adds to it for anyone who's looking. I went right to my classroom and wrote up a rebuttal complete with proof our department does silent reading as well as research about the benefits of giving students silent reading time in school. I reminded her of our AR program the district purchased to encourage more silent reading. As well, I spoke with several other English teachers in our department, and they were taken aback. I emailed her the document and walked a copy immediately to her office, but she was gone. This is my career, and she was about to tear up my reputation with this poor evaluation. My own poor children were waiting at home for me, but here I was, defending myself, again!

The next morning when I checked my email, there was an urgent one from the AP asking me to come to her office at my earliest convenience. It was a kind email, and I replied I would see her on my break. I brought my copies, just in case she was trying to claim she never got them. The second I sat down, she began to explain herself. She went on about what a terrible day it was yesterday and how she just wanted to relax in my room and watch me teach. She said she got my email and documents, and she pulled out her evaluation of me and laid it on the table. She said, "Jennifer, if you wouldn't mind, will you please bring your rebuttal and I'll meet you at the shredder with this evaluation?" What? I was a little confused but went with her to the office shredder. She asked me to put my rebuttal in the shredder right after she put my evaluation in. She said, "Let's pretend none of this happened and start fresh, please?" I'm not sure I can do that. She ruined my day and night, depriving my children of their mother for the afternoon and upsetting me for the night. I reminded her that this can be a redo, but it will not be forgotten. I kept all copies. I was very wary of her after that, and as it turns out, rightly so.

The Bee Situation

One morning as I was arriving early to school, an announcement came on the loudspeaker saying everyone on campus needed to get to the multipurpose room (cafeteria) immediately. Whoa? What was going on here already this morning? I gathered my things and made my way there along with other students and teachers. As the room was filling up, an announcement was made over the loudspeaker, "Attention, teachers and students! There was a bee attack on campus this morning, and the fire department has been called. Stay in the multipurpose room until we release you."

The multipurpose room (cafeteria) was designed to hold five hundred people comfortably, but there were over eight hundred students and seventy-five teachers in there now. The bell rang, and the school day officially began. We all watched through the windows as the fire truck made its way onto the campus, through the breezeway, and past the library. The students were pretty calm and collected as we waited for the announcement to head to our first-period classes. Approximately an hour later, we were all still crammed in here and tempers were starting to flare. We had a group of eighth-grade boys who were known to be troublemakers, all clumped by one of the railings in the cafeteria. Many of us teachers were watching them pretty closely, and their voices were getting louder and louder. It was loud enough in there, but this group was really starting to yell at each other.

Well into hour two, the boys decided they wanted to push each other. We asked them to calm down, but I'll admit, we were all getting tired of standing, crammed in here like sardines for the past few hours. It wasn't long before these boys were violently pushing each other into other students and falling down. There were teachers all around, and none of them were stepping forward to stop this action. NONE! I decided I would go ahead and step forward and address the problem. As I stepped toward the mass of boys, one of them decided to jump up on the railing and jump off into the crowd. As he jumped up from the ground, I leaned into this personal space, setting my hand on his shoulder and said, "I need you to calm down and be patient, like the rest of us."

He reacted like a ninja and leapt at my face saying, "I'll do what I want, bitch!"

I immediately leaned in more, and now that we were face to face, I said, "No, I am in charge and you WILL calm down." He backed off a little, and I relaxed. I might mention that when this was happening, not one teacher came behind me to help. He turned away and called me another choice name to his buddies while pushing one of them into the crowd again. I leapt forward into the mass of boys and pointed my finger. "I need you to come sit over here by the teachers until we get out of here." I pointed my finger at him then over by the wall.

He glared at me and, coming closer again, laughed. "Bitch, fuck off!"

I pointed my finger at him and said, "You better watch your mouth. Go over by the wall and sit down!"

He grabbed my hand, stepped his whole body within an inch of mine, and spit in my face. He also said, while spitting,

"Don't you ever put your finger in my face, bitch! I'll beat your face in if you ever do it again!"

I was shocked but kept calmly saying, "I asked you to stop, and I want you to go sit by the wall. You will stop talking to me like that and go sit by the wall." I was trying to keep cool, but inside I was screaming and wondering why not ONE male or female teacher came to help me. They were standing all around watching, along with hundreds of students, while this student spit and screamed at me. Seriously, not ONE teacher even stood behind me. I was secretly wishing he would hit me so I could beat him down in front of his friends. I was pumped and primed to let loose, but I knew he had to be the one to strike the first blow.

All of a sudden, a giant hand reached forward and grabbed this boy by the shoulders, lifting him off the floor and out of the building door. It was our vice principal who was six foot, six inches and easily three hundred pounds. He had been circulating about the room and saw what was going on. He parted the sea of students and took this student out. I immediately looked around at the other teachers and put my hands out saying, "Why didn't you help me?!" I shook my head and just stood there. Shortly thereafter, the bell rang, and the announcement was made to all head back to our second-period classes. For now, this ordeal was over, and little did I know, it was about to get worse.

The next day I came to school and found out that after being taken to the office that day, the boy who was cursing and spitting in my face was sent back to class before the end of second period without discipline. I open my email and find that I am to come up to the office as soon as possible. What now?? There is plenty of time left until the first bell, so I head up there right away. The principal's secretary tells me that he is busy but must talk with me as soon as possible. I tell her I'll come at my break, and I head back to class. I still do not know why he needs to see me but feel like it is going to be about the incident yesterday in the cafeteria. I am happy I am finally going to be defended, and they probably want to hear my side of the story before they discipline this boy. I certainly did not predict the chain of events which happened next.

The principal and vice principal were sitting there with grave faces as they waved for me to find a chair. I realized I was about the be questioned but not so I could tell my side of the story but so I will have to defend myself. Here are a sample of the questions:

"Why did you touch this boy?"

"Why did you feel it was necessary to approach him?"

"Why didn't you ask another teacher to assist you?"

"How many times did you grab this boy?"

Whoa, I told them! I began to tell my side of the story, and they said they did not care. They said the boy's mother called this morning, and she wanted to file legal charges against me for assaulting her son at the assembly yesterday. She was dead serious and said her son came home very upset saying I had attacked him and he wasn't doing anything. He said I grabbed him by the neck and pushed him to the ground.

I was then informed they did not want to talk to me anymore and this boy would not have consequences for screaming obscenities and spitting in my face. I asked them if they had spoken to any of the other teachers or students, and they said no. I was informed they had spoken to a few of the boy's friends who corroborated his story. They were going to decide what process they needed to go through to prosecute me for assault on this boy, as per the mother's wishes. I immediately told them they needed to hear my side of the story as well as talk to any of the twenty-plus other teachers who saw everything that happened.

I stormed out of the office and started making my rounds to these other teachers. I pleaded with them to come forward and defend me. Several of them said they weren't comfortable saying anything but good luck. Mind you, these teachers were in the room and saw the whole thing but simply didn't want to say anything. I find that is how teachers are; will fight for the kids but never one of our own. At last, I was able to convince one of the male teachers (yes, gender mattered) to come forward and give his account.

Shortly after, I got a call from the principal that the matter had been dropped and I was off the hook. They were not going to discipline the boy, but we are all going to pretend it didn't happen. A week later in another classroom, an older teacher's aide instructed this same boy to stop his disruptive behavior as he pointed his finger at him. This eighth-grade boy, who had been so combative with me and was not disciplined in any way for it, punched this man so hard in the face that he fell to the ground, hitting his head. This boy laughed and pointed and said, "Don't ever put your finger in my face or I'll punch you again!" Huh. Wonder if they disciplined him for that one?

Personal Space

We should all take a lesson from children. The media tells us bullying is so rampant in the schools that we have to have programs and training to deal with it. Yes, bullying exists and always will, and as adults, it is our job to monitor it and re-direct behavior. However, the opposite is true. If adults could just keep rules firm and give kids down time once in a while, they do pretty well. I sit in a percussion ensemble class at a high school, and after performing for me (I directed and led them as a sub, weren't they surprised?!), we are watching videos of other percussion ensembles performing at competitions. We are in a large room with a huge drop-down screen, and the kids are pretty much engaged. Some are on their phones (see phone section), but most are thumping to the beat. Why do I put this info in a section about personal space, you ask? Because as I look around the room, I see kids of different ages, colors, and genders singing together, leaning on each other, sharing info, sharing a hoodie as a pillow, lying on one another's legs, patting each other's heads to the beat and in general, enjoying each other with no worry for personal space. Nothing is inappropriate or uncomfortable, and if it ever is, these kids have no problem telling each other so.

The Whatever Generation

We've had so many generations defined throughout the ages like, baby boomers, Gen X, Gen Y, and even now Millennials, but I do believe that the youth today can be defined as the Whatever Generation (Gen W). Of course we now know they are called Gen Z but I still like to think of them as Gen W.

In my travels to different schools and having been teaching since 1996, I've seen the touchy-feely sentimentality grow and grow so much so that kids don't read anymore. I've always been so horrified when I'd see people say, "He graduated high school with the fifth-grade reading level" or stats about students graduating college who cannot read. Are we simply pushing kids through the system for the almighty dollar (asses-in-the-seats money). or do we feel so bad for kids that we coddle them into stupidity? I will use an example of this from a substitute job I did in August of 2016 in an eighth-grade classroom.

They were assigned to read "Ransom of the Red Chief" out of the textbook and answer questions in the back of the book, afterward. The teacher had left the audio version so the kids could listen and follow along. I've always despised this method as it allows kids to zone out, and many do not follow along. I eschewed the audio tape (much to the chagrin of the students) and forced them to take turns to read aloud. As soon as I said it, there was a howling and whining from the crowd. So many complaints about not wanting to read aloud, not being good at it, not being able to read…really? I told them too bad and proceeded to assign an order for around the room reading.

Immediately, I realized the problem with these kids and the progressions of education over the years as the first few kids struggled to follow proper sentence structure or properly pronounce simple words. They would breeze right over a period or comma without a pause, then stop reading or give pause when there was not one. This story was written in the early 1900s and used large words like progeny, diatribe, deleterious, and so forth. What began to happen is that as they come across words they do not know, they'd say, "Whatever." The word in parenthesis is the word in the text which they would jump right over. For example, here's a sentence from the story as the students read it: "At last, I fell into a (troubled) whatever sleep, and dreamed I had been (kidnapped) whatever by a (ferocious) whatever (pirate) whatever with red hair."

I stopped them and said, "You need to read the words."

He says, "I don't know them."

I replied, "Then you must try to sound them out and learn the words. This is school, and learning is key."

They refuse to try and say they never have to read aloud in class. What a shame! Thus because of teacher's refusal to call these kids to the carpet and force them to experience a little public discomfort, they are have become the "Whatever" generation. As a teacher, I hang my head in disbelief and shame.

Phones in class?

In today's classroom, the teacher has very little power. They are merely a "friend," babysitter, and curriculum guide. Teachers have been told by parents and administrators to leave the kids alone and allow them freedom to be themselves. Don't take, don't touch, don't look, don't ask! If they need to use their phones, we must assume it is for research or other needs. We are to allow them to text and talk on their phone for the sake of safety and communication with a parent. We are not to take or even look at their phones, as it could be considered theft or an invasion of privacy. We have been to training sessions going over the punishment we will endure if we breach their privacy or see a picture of them in a compromising position.

As I sit here subbing in a junior- and senior-level guitar class in the brand-new year of 2017, I realize it has been taken to a new level. The students are roaming in and out of the class, the halls are clogged with kids, and teachers are weaving in and out of them. I'm sitting in a theater room next door to a room where they are giving current eighth graders tours and talks. Some kids are helping, some are sitting in this room with me playing and singing all different songs, and kids from other classes are wandering in and out of the room. One of the girls who is wandering about decides someone took her guitar and is going to go look for it. She randomly answers her phone in the room, walks out of the room, talking to whoever called, and casually walks back in. She decides to look in the room where the eighth graders are and stops before opening the door. She says, "There's a bunch of eighth graders in the room where my guitar is. I don't want to set a bad example and be on my phone." At least she has some level of proper judgement even though she was just talking on it during class.

As well, one of the most valuable things to a student these days is a charger or source of electricity. They wander like lost children until they find someone who can loan them a charger or a nearby outlet. Many, many times I walk into a room to sub and there are phones charging along the walls. There are extra chairs in rooms, just to set charging phones on so no one accidently kicks the precious phone. It used to be that only a rare few children had phones, but now, EVERY student has a smart phone and is cruising the internet and taking photos all the time.

Reverse Racism, Plain Racism or Children Thinking They Know Better?

I go back and recall another class (2016), which was eighth-grade Language Arts subject but different teacher. This teacher's Honors class was reading *The House on Mango Street*. Here's the exact description: ***The House on Mango Street** is the remarkable story of Esperanza Cordero. Told in a series of vignettes – sometimes heartbreaking, sometimes deeply joyous – it is the story of a young Latina girl growing up in Chicago, inventing for herself who and what she will become.*

The lesson plan instructions were to play the audio CD, have the students follow along, then answer several questions on a three-page worksheet. As stated before, I am not a proponent of using the audio CD in place of having students read. I decided to ask them this time, unlike the other classes where I simply had them read aloud. My question was posed as such, "You all are honors students and are reading this novel. Please raise your hand and give me an honors quality reason why you like or dislike this novel."

Many hands were raised, so I called on a few. Various answers were, "I don't like it," "I think it's cute." And such. I reminded them that I was looking for an honors-type answer and continued to call on students. One boy I called on gave a measured, appropriate answer. "I do not like the book because I feel it is immature and does not make my imagination take interest." A girl close to him immediately raised her hand, so I called on her. It seemed she had something very important to contribute. She said, "Of course you don't like the book. You're white! You would never understand this character and have never lived like she has! You are white and just don't like reading about Hispanics!"

I stopped her as fast as I could and was upset at her rudeness. I said, "This is not a black, white, Hispanic thing. I asked you for an honors answer with your opinion about the book and you choose to attack another student about his answer. You are incorrect to assume his answer is racially based and need to think of a better way to address people." She was appropriately subdued, and I moved on to other students. I will go ahead and mention that the boy was fair with blond hair, and the girl was dark with dark hair. I will not assume he is white or she is Hispanic.

She eventually raised her hand again and I called on her. Her answer was finally about her opinion of the book, given in a thoughtful manner. She spent the rest of class not looking at me but did say good-bye when the bell rang. Have I helped or hurt the situation? I do know that as the only adult in the room, it is my job to direct their behavior and help them understand this is meant to be a non-threatening environment. After all, they are still children and learning, every day.

Sixth-Grade Language Arts - Fall 2011

All events from this school took place in the space of nine months.

I have always worked, even when my children were born and very small. After my divorce several years back, I met a wonderful, supportive man who knew how miserable I was teaching in the current middle school. We discussed it endlessly, and knowing he ran his own business and was self-sufficient, we agreed I would quit teaching and be a substitute teacher. However, I still held an enormous amount of guilt about not having consistent work and quietly continued to look for a contracted teaching job. I thought if I found the perfect job, I would jump on it. This would only be eighth- to twelfth-grade English at a private or charter school, and I applied at the Catholic diocese and several charter schools in my area. At this same time, I had a good friend who was the secretary at a school in the East Valley, and she always talked about what a great place it was to work. She told me about a sixth-grade English opening and asked if I was interested in interviewing? I said why not and gathered my courage to call and make an appointment.

The interview went great, and I really loved the principal and other teachers in the room. I was completely honest with them about my previous teaching experience and the situations I was put in based on the administration I was under. They admitted they had called him, and he did not have good things to say about me. I let them know I run a very military-style classroom and am tough on academics. My methods have always been seen as "old school," but I get results, and the kids respect me and learn. They seemed fun and easy going, and they offered me the job right away. I accepted the job because I felt I had laid everything on the line and there were no stones unturned in regard to me and my teaching style. When I told my friend I took the job, she was so excited and let me know how awesome the sixth-grade team was and how much I was going to love it!

As well as it went, and even though I accepted the job, I got to my car and burst into hysterical tears. I didn't understand why I was so upset! This was a good thing! Steady paychecks for the next nine months, medical benefits, more money in my retirement account, great people to work with, and one of my greatest friends right there for me to smile at every day. Why? Still, I spent the better part of this day crying and feeling depressed. I think deep down I knew I was not in a situation where I had the freedom to simply be a substitute teacher with no benefits or consistent work but real responsibility. Enough of this blubbering, so I straightened up and faced reality. Even though I did not want to be stuck in another bad teaching situation, my guilt won.

I began the arduous work of researching the Arizona state standards of sixth-grade Language Arts. I just came out of teaching seventh- and eighth-grade Language Arts. When I left the previous teaching job, I thought I was never going to be a teacher again as I was so soured on all of it. I had thrown out most of my books, teaching materials, and classroom decorations, but teaching sixh grade is a different bird. I would have to get new things anyway.

A few small details were left out of the conversation when I was interviewing for this job. For example, I was not told they intend to allow parents to dictate policies and grades. As well, they ignore the curriculum guidelines of the AZ state standards in favor of constant district testing. I was also not told that this was to be a one-year only job, as the sixth grade this year was so large, I was an add-on. The following year's grade (currently fifth) was small, so they would be shrinking back down to three teachers and getting rid of me. I did not learn that fact until March of 2012, when I did not get a contract for the following year. They knew that from day one, which makes the events of the year seem to make sense.

I also learned very quickly that this school was very unorganized and were focused solely on improving district test scores to compete with neighboring districts. They required weekly lesson plans be tied to the district testing guidelines, instead of the AZ state standards, and my plans were always tied to the state standards. They didn't like that one bit. I would tell them that the state standards are in the district tests, but the kids need to learn ALL the standards as it will benefit them in years to come. For example, the state standards dictate the students learn reading comprehension from several different genre of novels as well as short stories. However, when I decided to have the students read a district-approved novel as a class, I was called in to "talk" about my insubordination. I was told it didn't meet the district standards and never to do another novel. What? The district and state testing consist of vignettes and does not require context from an entire novel. Students will be reading novels in high school and college, so to remove them from the curriculum for the sake of achieving higher test scores is pure ridiculousness! If a student has a well-rounded education and is not constantly harped upon about testing, they will naturally do well.

Another thing the district wanted me to leave out was spelling and grammar. I was teaching a lesson on different types of nouns with worksheets (from the textbooks provided at the school), and this day I was having the students make a foldable. This was a folding activity where they made an accordion-like booklet that could be folded small and pulled out to be large. They were then required to write different types of nouns and draw a matching picture or write a sentence on each fold. Students loved this activity as it reached so many areas of their creative brain and helped them remember what nouns were. Unfortunately, this was also the day the principal decided to informally observe my teaching. She stayed and watched me demonstrate step by step as a class when to fold the paper so it would appropriately accordion in and out. At first glance it seems like chaos, but the kids were getting it! They were following directions, asking questions, laughing, and helping each other. She stayed for a few minutes, then left, shaking her head.

This same afternoon I received an email asking me to come to her office when I could. I went directly after school thinking she would be so happy I was creatively teaching the students. Boy, was I wrong! She admonished me for "wasting classroom time on a craft" and purposefully veering off the district standards. Thankfully, the state standards include teaching grammar, but she said that is irrelevant. She wrote all of this on the Informal Observation form and told me to sign it, giving me a bad evaluation. She informed me it will be in my permanent file. I would not sign it, but she told me it didn't matter. She will just put in my file that I was refusing. I asked if I was allowed to speak regarding my project with the students, and she said no. She'd seen enough to know it was a waste of class time. I couldn't believe it!

In October, schools have parent/teacher/student conferences. This is always a big production, and the school offers incentives to those grades who pull in the most parents to attend. We are to have a meeting before school to strategize as a staff, then meet as a grade level to strategize how to pull the parents in. What a waste of time! I could certainly spend my time more wisely doing research, create lesson plans, or even go home and see my own children. Teachers must meet outside of our paid workday. Teachers do not get extra pay for staying late for conferences, coming early for meetings, meetings on our lunch and break, school dances...it is just part of the job and is accepted.

We do so many things on our own time for zero extra pay on a barely livable salary. The icing on the cake is that parents expect teachers to do things for them on their own time. They actually get mad when you cannot stay after to talk to them about their child on any given day and say things like, "I'm a taxpayer and I pay your salary." Or "You work for me." Or "Quality...fair and equal...I deserve..." Teachers love to hear that. It motivates us into opening up our hearts and time for your child. Plus, I'm pretty sure that most if not all parents handsomely reward their child's teachers with gifts and money, every year. I hope you suspect sarcasm here.

Teaching sixth grade is a challenge because they are too old to be babies, they think they know everything, and they are too young to be completely trusted to make proper decisions. Many times, the parents become almost friends with us teachers because we learn info about their children that they cannot get. In this case, I had a mother who was growing ever concerned with her daughter's behavior at home. She had become sullen and no longer wanted to talk to the girl who had been her best friend since she was small.

The school had assigned the sixth grade to conduct our conferences in the Social Studies room, all together but at different tables for privacy. FERPA (Family Educational Rights and Privacy) dictates we are not allowed to talk about a student to another student or family, in any way. This classroom was a standard size, with one teacher in each of the four corners of the room. There were parents waiting with their kids all over the room as well as the parents and kids in the corners trying to talk to the teachers. This mother sat down at my table and in a very hushed tone asked me who her daughter plays with at school. Very quietly, I said, "There is one girl who is not the best choice..." but told her that's all the info I could give. She nodded her head as if she understood and said she will probe her daughter further and thank you very much.

She said, "I know I can trust you."

I said, "Always."

The room was chaotic with noise, people talking, little ones running about, and it certainly wasn't private, but we were told to do this, so we did.

The next day I got an email asking me to come to the office on my break. Ugh, I sure was getting tired of being called into the office. When I got there the principal and AP were waiting for me with papers on a table. I sat down and played it cool. "What's up?" I asked casually.

"We have written you up for violating FERPA and talking about a student to another parent. Sign here."

Um, no, I will not. "May I at least read this and have you tell me what proof you have?"

"We had a parent tell us she overheard you talking to another parent about someone else's kid. We just need you to sign this."

I replied, "That's your proof? What name did I say? Who was I talking about? What parent was I with at the time? How do you know I wasn't with this kid's mother? You don't even want an account from my side? I'll tell you I know the rules, and I NEVER tell anyone about someone else's kid. Well, if you are not letting me say anything to defend myself, I am not signing this." Again, they didn't care and wrote down I refused to sign. They let me know this was grounds for termination and I better watch myself. This is harassment! I am the victim here, and I cannot believe in my multiple years of being a teacher, I am being treated like a criminal. I walked out of there and went back to my class. Mind you, this was two months into a nine-month school year, and already I'm being threatened constantly. It sure is motivating!

The Science Trip

The sixth-grade class of this school goes on an annual science trip up north, for a few days during the school week. This is an overnight with parents, teachers, and kids and is planned months ahead through before- and after-school meetings as well as a night meeting for parents to attend. Of course, we do not get extra money for any of this time outside the school day, and it is mandatory to attend. The three other sixth grade teachers decided without asking me during lunch time that I would not go on the science trip because, and I quote, "It doesn't seem like you're into it and want to go." I said no, I do not want to go and would rather stay home with my children instead of finding someone to take them for a few days as well as find a dog sitter. I did say, if I had to go, I would and make the best of it. The sixth-grade science teacher was pregnant and said she really didn't want to go either but guesses she has to if I won't go. I told her if she can't go, I certainly will, and she kind of shrugged me off.

In the weeks leading up to the trip (it was in November), the kids started asking me why I wasn't going. They clamored for me to please go, but I told them the other three teachers have it handled. I told them I'd love to go, but I have to stay behind and take care of the students who cannot go and come to school. I have my real feelings, but I told the kids I'd love to go so I wouldn't hurt their feelings. I thought they understood, but soon after that I got another email telling me to come to the office at my break. Really? What now?

I went to the office on my break, instead of grading papers or making copies or calling/emailing parents, because I was told to. The principal and AP were waiting for me at the table with papers, again. This time they started by asking me why I said nasty things about the other sixth-grade teachers in front of the students? What? I said I never said anything nasty about the other teachers and certainly not in front of the students. They said, "We've had some kids come to us and say you said it wasn't fair you couldn't go on the science trip and the other teachers excluded you on purpose. We talked to several other students, and they all say the same thing. We need you to sign these papers for your permanent file saying you are insubordinate."

I replied, "Whoa, wait, do you want me to tell you my side of the story and how these kids are wrong? You are going to take the word of the children over a forty-one-year-old, veteran teacher, without question?"

They said, "Just sign these papers and stop talking about the other teachers to the students."

At this point, I was beginning to not care one little bit about this school or the kids or anything and I signed it. Who cares anymore?

The Insubordinate Student

I found out through talking with other teachers (other grades) in the teacher's lounge that the current year's sixth-grade class is the worst this school has ever seen. They told me I was thrown into the fire because the admin knew how bad these kids are. They lie, steal, curse, cheat, and the parents think they are angels. Not all of them, mind you, because that would be silly, but I am generalizing. I have many kids in the five classes of twenty-five to thirty who misbehave, blurt things out, yell, try to hurt other students, talk back to me, and need constant discipline. One boy has to sit in the back, and he acts sullen every time I try to talk to him. The mother is no help and has told me to do whatever I want with him because she can't. I have another boy whose parents recently split up and he has refused to do anything in class and threatens to kill himself. I have a girl with a very bad attitude and bad reputation with the boys and girls for being sexually graphic. When I conference with her mother, the mother tells me her daughter is NOT like that and to quit making up lies. The mother comes to conference in the tightest dress, high heels, and cleavage popping out. I'll say no more.

However, I also have one student who thinks he is extremely special and doesn't have to do a darn thing I say, ever. He fights with me every day and refuses to sit in his assigned seat until I get loud with him. When I ask him to sit in his seat he says, "Why?" When I ask him to get out his homework he says, "Why should I?" When I ask him where his pencil or homework is he says, "I don't care." I can handle this, but when he won't sit in his assigned seat and I press him, he fights. He throws his books down, tips over the chair and yells, "I don't like that seat!" Meanwhile, I'm trying to get the other twenty-five-plus students settled in after the bell, take attendance, field fifty questions (every day), and get them started on their warm-up exercise.

I've stopped teaching a few times and called this boy's mother, but she tells me to deal with it; he is fine at home. I feel so bad for the other students who lose their teacher for five minutes or so, almost every day, while she deals with this one boy. I finally decide I need to write him up for his bad behavior after four months of fighting with him and giving him chances to straighten up. I've taken him out in the hall to talk to him, and he yells in my face. He's tried every nerve I have and I'm referring him to the office. I get out the paperwork, and the kid laughs at me. I call the office to tell them I'm sending him with referral papers, and they say okay. I hand him the papers and send him off with his things.

He is gone for most of class and then returns with a smirk on his face. I call the office and ask them why he is back, and they say he came but didn't have any paperwork with him, so they sent him back. I am flabbergasted and ask why they didn't call me. I can send it with another student to make sure it gets there, and they tell me not to bother. They talked with him, and he seems fine, so all is well. All is well? No, I say, all is not well. I hang up the phone, get the kids working again, and go talk to the boy. He's calm and quiet and smiling a big "I ate the canary" smile. I ask him what happened to his referral papers, and he says, "I do not know. I gave it to them, but they threw it out and sent me back." For some odd reason, I actually believe him. I feel crazy for thinking that, but I do sort of believe him. I start to think I'm losing my mind and question myself. I re-write the referral paper, set it in my desk drawer, and decide to let the day go by and deal with it later.

Before school the next day, there is an announcement for me to report to the office. Oh boy, here we go. I knew that other shoe would drop eventually. I grab that referral paper and head up to the office. It is getting close to the bell ringing for the day, and I encounter one of our aides looking for me. She says, "I've been assigned to watch your class while you are in the office". Okay, I say. Now I'm totally confused and brace myself for a fight. I get to the office and am shooed into a conference room, where seated at a big, oval table is the principal, AP, mother, student, and school counselor. Huh, the firing squad this time. Wonder what I did wrong to be ambushed like this?

I smile and take a seat while the principal turns to the mother and asks for her side of the story. I quietly wonder why she even has a "side" to the story as she wasn't there in the room. However, I patiently sit and wait for my turn. The mother is furious at the way her son is being treated and said he came home last night crying and saying I humiliated him in front of the class. She said he told her I yelled at him and all the kids heard it. She says that he told her he didn't do anything wrong and that I'm out to get him and I attack him, every day. She looks at her son several times throughout this account and he nods fairly consistently. He steals glances at me here and there, and I just smile at him.

The principal now turns to me and asks me to explain why I sent this student to the office yesterday. I now produce the referral I duplicated to replace the one which was "lost" on the way to the office or thrown away. I pass it around the table and ask them all to read what it says. The principal asks why she doesn't have a copy of this, and I say, "I do not know. I sent it to the office with the student yesterday and he said it was thrown away." She looks at the student, and he nods yes. She looks at me and asks why I didn't follow up, and I said I did but was told not to worry about it. As this is going on, the mother is becoming more furious, and the boy is growing more smug.

The mother starts to fume and asks the principal what she's going to do about this. She looks at me and says, "My son doesn't like you, and I always taught him to fight if he feels he's being treated poorly." The principal intervenes and turns to me asking me to explain the exact events. Even though they are detailed in the referral, I give a shortened version of the yelling, insubordination, rudeness, disruption, throwing of books, and knocking over chairs. The mother tries to interrupt me, but I keep talking only louder. I look right into her eyes and say, "Your son refuses to do what is asked of him in class." As she starts to say something in return, I turn to the boy and ask him, "Do you do what I ask when you come in the room?" He stammers, looks away, and says no. I ask him, "Do you fight with me when you refuse to sit in your assigned seat, almost every day?" He looks away again and says yes. I ask him, "Do you throw your books or backpack down and tip over chairs when you do not want to cooperate in class?"

He puts his head down and shouts, "Yes but I don't want to sit where you put me in class. I want to sit by my friends!"

I look right into the mother's eyes and say, "Your son is rude and refuses to cooperate in class, every day. He takes away from the other students' learning time because I have to handle him. I've called you, and you tell me to deal with it. Here is the referral, do with it what you wish." I look at the principal and say, "You all have taken away from the rest of my students today and I'm going back to my room to teach." I walk out of the room and back to my classroom. I am flushed, upset, and nervous about the repercussions coming to me from this morning. Sadly, I am caring less and less about being a teacher or these students. It makes me feel desolate and lost inside.

The Teacher Parent

One of the most difficult beasts to work with, when you are a teacher, is the teacher-parent. The absolute worst is when the teacher-parent works at the same school as you and their child is in the same building, close to the same grade. This girl's mother was a seventh-grade teacher while I was teaching sixth grade, and her daughter was in one of my classes. Please remember I had five classes of thirty students throughout every day. Her daughter was a lovely, sweet, caring girl who was really trying hard to study and excel but simply couldn't get there without a lot of help. The girl likes me and often tells me about her mom and new stepdad. She tells me they spend all of their time together, and she barely sees her mom. She tells me about how busy she is and how she stays up late to do homework but gets really tired. I seem to think the mother wanted her daughter to get all of her work and studying done in the school day so that she could focus on after-school sports and activities in the evenings, but I'm not sure.

According to The Arizona State Standards of Teaching and I believe that students should learn how to "chunk" words to gain greater knowledge of their meaning as well as spell, use in a sentence, and define words. I used a workbook series called *Greek and Latin Roots and Stems*. For example, the word bilateral would be broken down so they understood that *bi* means two and *lat* means side. They then understood the word means, two-sided. There were words like, bicycle, biped, and so on. Each week we learned a new stem and root and had a wall in the room where we did activities, and they used the Root Wall to match items.

This girl really struggled with spelling, meanings, and constructing sentences for these words. Every week she would half do her homework and then fail the quiz. She was allowed to redo her homework and retake the quiz but rarely finished the homework or retook the quiz. I would get to class early or stay later after school to help her, but she still failed. Her grade was falling, and her mom (teacher-parent) was growing ever concerned. She came to me a couple of times, and we discussed strategies. I told her I could waive a few of the quizzes, but the homework had to be done to completion. I reminded the mother that if her daughter would simply work on and complete the homework throughout the week, she will do better on the quizzes. I also reminded her that I give the students ample time in class to work and ask questions all week long, and her daughter simply sits there and stares at other students. She kept saying she will talk to her daughter, and we agreed to allow her to continue to redo work to raise her grade.

Without warning one morning, I got an email saying after school today, I must come to the office to address a parent concern. Huh. I wonder which parent has a problem now and why they didn't come to me but go right to the principal. I traipse there after school, and lo and behold, the teacher-parent was sitting there with the principal. She and the principal have known each other for several years, and I was the newbie. They were pleasantly chatting when I entered the room, so I smiled and sat happily down. Immediately, the mood went somber, and the principal began. "We called you in here today because it seems you are unwilling to work with Mrs... . daughter to have her become successful in your class."

I began to fume internally but still smiled. I looked directly at the teacher parent and said, "Oh, haven't I been working with your daughter, and haven't you and I had several meetings regarding her progress and shortcomings?"

The mother looked at the principal and said, "Yes, but it just isn't enough". I will remind the reader that I have over 150 students every day. I do not want that to be an excuse but simply a thought. A reminder, if you will.

The principal looked at the teacher parent and said,

"Jane, what exactly is the problem here?"

Teacher-parent calmly says, "I have been doing research and the program she's using doesn't contain anything that's on the district or state testing. I do not think she should be teaching it as it is unfair." I begin to state that over ninety-five percent of the students in my classes are progressing nicely and learning very well, but I was shut down.

"Is this true, Jennifer?" asked the principal. I asked them both to refer the AZ state standards and guidelines for sixth-grade Language Arts, where it clearly states the students should learn how to deconstruct words using roots and stems. They both ask me to refer to the district testing standards, where nothing is mentioned about grammar, vocabulary, roots, or stems. I ask them why they are not interested in a well-rounded student as they will need to know these things for high school? They both look at each other, and the principal tells me to stop teaching Greek and Latin roots and stems. I am flabbergasted! Are you kidding me? I've been successfully teaching students how to deconstruct words to gain greater meaning for the past many years. Students learn so much from this, and I am being told by the "leader" of the educators at this school to STOP teaching something that's on the AZ state standards. All I can say is, wow.

The teacher-parent wins, and the only loser is the student. Actually, all of my 150-plus students lose in this war. Bravo.

Why does anyone become a teacher?

Media Spin on Teaching

I was talking to a friend of mine one day about a local election race for an open seat in the Senate. She is family friends with one of the candidates and wanted to tell me about one of the other candidates who she felt was not running for the right reasons. The other candidate is a younger man who has many (nine) small children and is running for US Senate, where he will be living part-time in DC and part-time in AZ, if he wins. She overheard him telling another person that he wanted to win because he needed more money to support his family. It turns out to be factual, and he has told that to many people. She felt that he should stay home with his wife and many small children and be a father, then down the road, run for Senate. She says he is running for all the wrong reasons, and a person should have a calling and not worry about the money. She then went on to say, "Like a teacher...they are not teachers for the money but because they love children and have a calling to teach. They know that teaching does not pay well and do not mind because they are doing what they love."

Right then and there I thought I MUST write this book to dispel the myths and open the public's eyes to what it really means to be/come a teacher. I did tell her she is wrong on so many levels, and she argued with me.

A conversation I recently had with another friend was regarding a teacher shortage, teachers walking off the job in the first few weeks, and lowering numbers of students wanting to become teachers. She linked it all to pay and felt satisfied with her answer. I am always honest with people, and I realize it will not always make some happy to hear harsh truths, but I move forward anyway. I explained to her that I've seen teachers walk off the job and knew many who were counting the days until their contract was over so they could leave the profession.

When a teacher accepts a job and signs their contract, they are fully aware of the pay scale and job at hand (unless they are a new teacher, then they know the pay and probably have no idea of the scale of work involved). Dissatisfaction due to low pay is a media-driven myth to generate more money for schools. Money of which almost never reaches the teachers either in higher pay or supplies for the classroom. A common perception is that teachers pay out of pocket to decorate their room and have office supplies. However, this is not the reason they leave either.

I proceeded to explain to my friend the reason I left teaching was due to crushing bureaucracy, incessant testing, and a basic "Big Brother" attitude toward teachers. Parents and students act entitled to whatever they feel is a quality education and treat teachers like slaves. They make statements like, "I pay taxes, so I basically pay your salary" or "You work for me." The administration (principals et al) does not always back the teachers and commonly believe everything the parents and students say with no regard for the truth or the teacher's testimony. There have been many times in my career where I had a student go home and tell their parents an overblown perception of how they were treated in the day, and the parent comes to the school angry and wanting my head on a platter. The principal merely allows this and calls the teacher in to be harshly admonished with little care to their side of the story.

I knew the pay was paltry, but I was also able to have medical and dental benefits, weekends and holidays off with my kids, and be there for them in the evenings and summers. I was willing to make the sacrifice, but was it a calling?

Over and over, I told my friend stories about teachers who were experienced and left not because of pay but the way they were treated and no longer allowed to teach content but only test prep. If teaching is a calling, then the general public, the media, and even the schools themselves are destroying that desire to follow their passion. Teaching is becoming a dead art. **We should now call it "administering."**

REFLECTION

Are students behaving better or worse over the years?

Regarding the school environment, are they better or worse?

When I started teaching, the kids in school were pretty poorly behaved. It was up to me (all teachers) to teach them how to behave in class but also, as per the administration, how to behave with each other and at home. You see, fewer and fewer parents are teaching their children how to behave at school. They raise them and laugh when they are "stubborn," "opinionated," "wild," "high energy," or even "mouthy." They don't seem to understand that that amusing behavior does not serve them well once they get out of the house. They shuffle them off to school and walk away. Then they act shocked when their little darling has behavior issues and must be more harshly disciplined. Parents must be called into the classroom/office and have it explained to them that it is not acceptable for Johnny to have a rude remark for everything the teacher says. It is not acceptable to lay under the desk. It is not acceptable to throw your things all over the desk and have a messy pit for a backpack. It is not acceptable to talk while the teacher is talking or during silent reading. It is not acceptable to say no when you are asked to start an assignment or fold your paper into an airplane because you think it's cute. The list goes on and on. This creates a huge problem for the teacher, which cuts into educational time, as now the teacher must spend time dealing with your child while the others wait.

It used to be that the percentage of unruly children in a classroom was one to five percent but now, the one to five percent are the kids actually wanting to learn and behave, while the rest socialize, refuse to get work done, and cause a whole host of problems through distraction tactics. Cute at home? I think not. A teacher's job of teaching your child a complex curriculum of information so they can be well-read, studious, and succeed to move on to college is a task which shouldn't be made more difficult by an adorable trouble-maker whose parents refuse to enforce discipline.

Are teachers bipolar? Bipolar education? Do we drive the students crazy or prepare them for the real world?

Ethics

Substitute Work and Pay

What keeps a substitute from walking out of the door when it gets hard in class? I know a teaching contract keeps the teacher in the classroom day after day, but a substitute signs no such deal. Subs agree to be present if they accept a position and understand that if they do not accept enough jobs or do not show up for too many jobs, they can be fired. A substitute used to have at least a bachelor's degree, obtain a substitute certificate from the Department of Education, and get a fingerprint clearance card from the Department of Public Safety (DPS) and be cleared by the FBI. A fingerprint clearance card can only be obtained by going to a local police station, where one must pay the police to physically fingerprint you and submit the prints and form to DPS. The wait time is about two to four weeks, and oftentimes they get kicked back for incomplete prints. This is an exhausting and expensive process and must be renewed every few years. The pay can range from eighty to two hundred dollars per day, depending on the school district, and most days are seven to nine hours. Although many subs are very old, read the paper, grump at the kids and sleep, most subs at least show up, so there is rarely disciplinary action. Kids can be very terrible to subs, but it is all in the attitude when you walk in the door.

Teacher Turned Sub

After leaving the contracted position of a teacher, I became a substitute teacher to keep my skills and brain fresh, although I initially planned to never return to the profession.

<u>SUBBING INTRO</u>

Being a substitute teacher is a noble art, yet you are often disregarded as a glorified babysitter. Kids do not respect you, teachers think you are fools, and the office staff treats you like you're retarded. In any case, there are many reasons I became a substitute instead of a full-time, contracted teacher and even let my teaching certificate lapse. Among the reasons are stress and bureaucracy. As outlined in my many experiences as a certified teacher, I also left the profession because stress is the number-one cause of multiple sclerosis relapses.

I had been diagnosed with MS in 2010 and continued teaching full time, to the best of my ability, until 2012. I had a terrible relapse due to stress on the job and when I had to be hospitalized and then bed-ridden for a week, the staff and admin at my school didn't give a hoot. I had to have steroid infusions as I could barely walk, lift my right arm, or make a fist. I had been failing and exhausted for weeks before finally getting medical care, and although I alerted them to this, the admin only doubled down on pushing me.

My pay was docked for the week until I could prove I really had MS and was forced to bring in a doctor's note along with my MRI scans. Even then, they docked me a few days saying I was not allowed to take advantage of FMLA due to the fact I'd only been at that school less than a year. Despite the fact that I had been teaching in the state of AZ for many years, none of that applied.

After that relapse, my husband and I decided I would not take another teaching position and sub when I had good days. Here is a compilation of my subbing experiences and the discoveries I made along the way.

Boy's PE, Junior High

Yesterday morning (Monday) I was hired at a local school district to be a substitute teacher. This morning (Tuesday) at nine, I was officially in the system to begin accepting jobs. I figured that since most schools have started their day by now that I can relax and know today will not be the day I begin subbing. While relaxing and preparing to plan our evening meal, I received a call from the Sub Line. It was approximately 11:58, and the job started at 12:00! Oh boy, I had better get out of my pajamas and get moving. The job was for seventh/eighth-grade PE, so I guess I will dress casually. Within minutes, I pull on comfy khakis, a T-shirt, and tennis shoes and run out the door.

Thankfully, the junior high is five minutes from our house, so I was there rather quickly. When I walked into the office, they seemed surprised to see me. I told them I was here to sub for Mr. C's P.E. class, and I was taken to a back office. Apparently, they told Mr. C to call in for NO sub needed, but he did not. Even though I was excited to sub, I offered to go home as I live very close. "No, it is your time too and we'll keep you," they told me. She hands me the keys and a sub folder and off I go. The sub folder is chock-full of school info, and I find out that I'm not due to have students until 1:00. Whew! I have time to organize myself and know what I'm doing today.

I finally find the gym (I didn't know where it was as I'd never been here before), and I look for an office or somewhere I can find directions or lesson plans. There was an office in the girl's locker room but not for Mr. C. Of course, dummy! The boy's PE teacher's office is probably in the boy's locker room, and I'm probably not allowed in there. Fine. I poke around in the girl's locker room PE teacher's offices and find nothing. I decide to wait in the gym in case a teacher happens by. One of the male PE teachers walks by and I all but wrestle him to the ground to get info. He tells me I can go hang out in the girl's locker room and he'll handle it. Um, no, I'm here and I can handle it. He says okay, but his class is playing football. "Can you play football?" Can I play football? Well, no, but I KNOW football and have three teenage sons, so yes!

He says fine and that he'll handle the warm-up, then I can take them outside. Cool!

I chat with the female PE teacher a bit, and then the kids come in. We begin with seventh-grade boys. They walk in and immediately play basketball. This other Coach blows his whistle and yells at my students to sit. They do but still mess around until I yell at them and assert myself. I have no idea what the discipline program is here at this school, but I know myself, and I'm not worried.

Calisthenics begin and I catch on quickly. I'm not young and in shape, but I can hold my own to show an example. Some of the boys think it's funny to NOT do what the coach says and just lay there during leg lifts. I plop myself on the ground and begin doing them. A few boys see me and start doing it. The ones who don't, I berate by saying, "Look at me! I'm an old, out-of-shape lady and I can do it, why can't you?" They all start participating, and the ones who still refuse are sneered at by the others. I will tell you, these boys were young and healthy and perfectly capable. I'm sure some of you readers are probably thinking, *she shouldn't force them to do it, what if they are hurt or not strong enough?* Nonsense! They were fine, just refusing to participate out of spite.

When we finally head outside to play football, I immediately establish myself as a linesman as they line up in teams. The game goes pretty smoothly as they realize I know this game very well and am officiating fairly. I don't know one kid from the other, so they have a clean behavior slate with me and know it. We all have so much fun! Don't get me wrong, a few boys test me by pushing and playing dirty, but I get to them, and they stop quickly. The game ends in a twelve-to-twelve tie. We weren't kicking extra points, so they were six-point touchdowns. The boys moan and groan about it being a tie and I tell them, "You know what a tie is, right?" They say no, so I tell them, "A tie is like kissing your sister!" Ewwwwww, they get grossed out, but we all laugh and joke all the way back to the locker rooms.

The next class is all eighth-grade boys and they file in very noisily. It starts like the other class, where the coach blows his whistle and gets them to sit in the bleachers so I can take attendance. These boys are a bit more obnoxious and rowdy, and they refuse to sit quietly. Again, I must break out my mom/teacher voice, only now I need to be more aggressive. NOW I have their attention! I haltingly begin calling names for attendance and have to stop often to stop them from climbing all over the bleachers, on each other, fluffing each other's hair, and asking me random senseless questions. So frustrating! I remind them that I am in charge and if they want to go outside to play football, they better behave and listen.

Coach blows his whistle and calisthenics begin. These kids do the same thing as the seventh graders and do not take it seriously. I walk over to the group of boys who think it is very amusing to make jokes and ignore the coach and me. I lay right next to them and do the exercises this coach is calling out. They stop and stare at me then keep lying there. I decide to challenge them by asking if they are all tired today. "Feeling weak? Is this too hard for you all?" The mumbling continues but is starting to fade. A few boys now start doing the exercises and try harder. They are laughing at me but doing it! I say, "Come on, boys, you can certainly beat an old lady?!" My legs were shaking, and my abs (or lack thereof) were burning, but I outlasted them, and they were impressed. We all jumped up, grabbed the football, and dashed outside!

Although I was pretty sure they had pre-assigned teams, they still ran around and created five minutes of melee and confusion. Again, I established myself as a linesman, and they fell into line. They were impressed I knew the game, and things went well. Unfortunately, there's always one or two students who feel they are better than the others and act like jackasses. One boy felt he was an NFL player who could tackle instead of grab the flag of a runner. The first time he tackled, I penalized his team five yards and told him if he did it again, he would be out of the game. This kid did it again, only this time he hit the other kid so hard, he hit his head on the ground. Of course, the tackler denied it and started making excuses, all of which indicated he did not feel bad for the kid he hit, at all. His denials were falling on deaf ears as some kids are huddling around the injured boy, and many, including myself, saw the whole thing. I instruct some kids to take the boy to the nurse, and I march over to handle the offender. I was telling him to go to the nurse as well and tell her that it was he who had hurt this kid, and he began to get angry at me. As he started walking away, he was turning back to look at me, cursing and yelling about how none of this was fair. I got in his face and asked him if he wanted ME to walk him up to the office, and he mumbled more quietly but said no. He continued mumbling and cursing all the way back to the building.

Behavior Decisions in the Class

May I explain this situation's demographics to those of you who may think I could have handled it differently? Allow me to set the scene. There were thirty-seven students in this PE class, but I've known some PE classes to have as many as fifty students to one teacher. Large PE classes are the norm in a public school, as it's an elective and is not regulated or limited by the state or district. As soon as all of us left the main gymnasium, we walked about twenty yards out to the edge of the field. The field is about fifty yards in length, and we were easily in the middle of that when the incident occurred. I was not given a walkie-talkie or even a phone number I could use my cell phone to contact anyone in the office. I am alone out on a field with thirty-seven thirteen- to fourteen-year-olds and must manage them all. I suppose I could have walked them all with me to the office, but that is punishing the whole for the transgression of one and, in this case, would not have been beneficial. See, I'm not sure if parents/the general public are aware of the daily crossroads and hard decisions teachers must make in an instant. Accidents are going to happen, kids are going to hurt each other, and feelings are going to be bruised.

After the chaos died down, we resumed the game at hand, and it went rather well. Right before the ongoing game was over, the offending student returned to the field. I assumed correctly he wasn't punished, and I would not let him re-join the game. I found it so very interesting how much effort some of these kids put into protesting their transgression instead of just understanding they made a poor choice, apologize, and move on. It is so much like a battle of wills, which, at this young age, should be fruitless. I am the adult in charge, and I win. The boys were very respectful and helpful as we ended the period and headed back into the gym. Many of them thanked me, and it was a pleasant ending. My guess is the other boys were tired of the bully boy always getting to do what he wanted with impunity and no one actually disciplining him. Who knows but I'd like to think that was their thought process. My day was over and after only two periods of subbing boys' PE and I was exhausted!

I ventured back into the girls' locker room to find the female coach to say good-bye. She was so pleasant and friendly as she asked for my phone number in case she needed a sub. I walked back to the office to return my folder and keys, and not one person spoke to me. I would think that after the injury and offending boy I sent up to the office, they would be looking to speak with me, but I was greeted with silence. Huh. I guess it wasn't a big deal. I know if it were my son as either the transgressor or injured party, I would have wanted a statement from the only adult to see it all happen. Guess not. I wasn't expecting a party after I endured this sub job, but a simple good-bye would have been nice. Oh well, they were busy, and I was tired, so perhaps I'll be back another day.

5:20 a.m.- High School, Advanced Physics

Snow. I'm sleeping on snow! *Shwoosh*, I go down the snowy sidewalk and I crash into a ringing bush. Ringing bush? I wake up and realize it's 5:20 a.m., and the sub line is calling me. Do I want a job today? Sleep sounds better, but I go ahead and answer the phone. This job offer is high school Honors Physics from 7:00 a.m. to 2:30. I decide to accept this mission! I am an English teacher who will substitute teach not only the strange and mysterious world of physics but at the honors level. Piece of cake! Well, maybe not, but I better go get ready.

I proceed to get my "uniform," of khaki pants and whatever solid-colored, flesh-covering clean shirt is available, and get moving. I have woken my husband who decided he may as well start his day. Sigh of contentment… I realize there are only dregs of coffee, which is two days old but warm it up anyway. I gather food in the form of left-over tuna, a few scoops of yesterday's pasta salad, crumbs of sugar cookie, and a scoop of five-day-old Brussel sprouts with green beans. I kiss my husband, and off I go. I didn't have time to fully get ready but figure I'll visit the bathroom when I get there and have a break. NOTE: this turns out to be a bad choice.

I pull up to the high school and hope I'm in the correct parking lot. I have zero clue where I'm going, so I head into the main door. Walking tall and assured, I enter the gorgeous, spacious entry where there is a twelve-foot Christmas tree complete with ornaments, lights, and bows. The administration offices are through a door to the right, where it is clean and quiet with many offices. I am directed to the sub coordinator/athletic director whose office is fifteen doors down.

The sub coordinator hands me a key and a piece of paper with the teacher's name and schedule on it. His schedule does not make any sense as the start times are not the same as the normal bell schedule times. As well, I notice he has zero breaks. She sends me on my way without another word (actually, she hands me the key and schedule and completely ignores me). I exit her office and enter the spider web of a campus where students are beginning to enter for the day. I was not given a folder, school rules, procedures, or map of the campus, so I know I'm on my own. I wrangle a custodian for directions and find the classroom.

I enter the physics room, which was incredibly cluttered. Half of the room is a woodworking shop, and the other half is white boards and desks. The woodworking shop is littered with sawdust, pieces of wood, computers, saws, drills, paint cans, and sandpaper, and it seems the kids are making guitars. The classroom half has about thirty desks and tables and a teacher's desk completely covered with stuff. I kid you not, I cannot even find a small space to put my cup of coffee. There were piles and piles of student papers, printed emails, stretched out Slinkys, screws, glue guns, wood filler, wire, calculators, miniature cars, batteries, composition books, old rags, bolt cutters, textbooks, springs, goggles...I could go on. I searched for a pen or pencil to take attendance with and there wasn't anything. On the floor, surrounding the desk, were piles and piles of student projects, textbooks, and graded/not graded student homework and tests. Aside from that, there was a layer of dust on everything.

The day's plans are handwritten in marker on a half-sheet of paper, and for six periods of classes, there are two sentences. Classes are fifty-six minutes long and they are to work on a two-page study guide for finals the following week. Oh boy, I don't know how high school students can work on a two-page assignment for an hour and stay on task in a classroom brimming with tools, wood, paint and chemicals all around them. Okay, then. Oh, and there are dust bunnies everywhere...ah-choo!

I give my spiel to the class and demand they work in relative silence. While I speak, the kids are great, and I realize they will be no problem. However, once attendance was done and I start to figure out what their task is, the chatter begins. Cell phones pop up, kids color on themselves and each other, paper is flicked, hair gets braided, novels are read, relationships are hashed out, the quiet kids retreat into themselves, and the loud ones make sure everyone can hear them. Once I pass out the study guide, they get to work, and I have nothing to do. I brought a book but hate to read in front of the students.

This teacher's schedule is not posted anywhere, nor does it say anything in the two sentences of directions the teacher leaves for me. I do not know how many classes I have, I do not know when my lunch is, I do not know when my break is, and I do not know where the bathrooms are. After first period ends, the next class files in. After that, third-period class files in and so on. It seems my decision to not use the bathroom before class started for the day was a bad choice and I begin to get desperate. I drank an entire cup of coffee and sips of my water, and my bladder is bursting! Between periods one and two I try to race through the crowded halls to find any bathroom. I wander, with no luck, and, as the bell rings, run back to the room to start the next class. I search again between periods two and three, but this time I slip into another teacher's room to ask where the bathroom is. She directs me to go three hallways over, make a right, and go by the office. I'm to ask the secretary if I get lost. What? Lost? You're kidding, right? I only had five minutes between classes and am now down to one with no bathroom and a bursting bladder. I happen by an ajar door and realize I hit pay dirt. I duck in quickly as the bell starts to ring. NO! I finish and RUN back to the classroom. I later found out that that bathroom is for the little kids whose nursery room is next door. That's why it was propped open.

When I returned to the room it was a good four minutes after the final bell and kids were everywhere. It was quite loud in the room, and I think they assumed I wasn't coming. Kids were sitting on desks, milling about, and yelling. I went barreling full speed into the room, went straight for the teacher desk, grab the attendance sheets, and ready my best mom/teacher voice. Success! Amid the moans and groans, they sit down and get quiet, mumbling, "Oh man!" Shortly, I have to call the office to find out what the rules are about cell phones in class as everyone had theirs out. They tell me to take them away if the kid refuses to put it away. I issue warnings, and the kids comply calmly. I find out that lunch is at 12:12, and I cannot wait to head back to the bathroom! I've been in class for four and a half hours and need a break. This teacher has a packed schedule! They should tell you that on the recording when you accept the job.

The last class of the day is engineering. They are making guitars, and I have been given a one sentence directive by the teacher: "Need to use drills in back to work on their guitars paint in drawer." Right away they get to work, and I hear power tools. They are using power saws, belt sanders, table saws, and spray paint. I am shocked they would allow these kids to use these tools with a sub here but okay. These kids have been pretty well-behaved today, and I wouldn't mind coming back even though the room is an utter disaster zone.

Ninth/Tenth-Grade Social Studies, High School- Mr. G

I accepted this job yesterday on the computer. It says to start at 6:55 a.m., so I get up early and head out. When I arrive, no one is in the sub coordinator's office, but the schedule and key is on the table. I grab it and think possibly I'll come talk to her later. I find the room after walking all over this massive campus, only to realize it's on the second floor! I get prepared before the bell rings and wait. The bell rings, and no one comes in. I wait and wait and no students. I glance at the schedule given to me and it says I do not have a first period. As this is a block day and classes are two hours long, I realize my first class will not arrive until 9:45. It is currently 7:25 and I'm not happy. I decide to head down to the office to see if I can leave for a few hours.

When I get down by the office, I see a wall of fence between the halls and front doors. There will be no leaving today unless I go through the office. I need to mention that there are over thirty-six hundred students in the school and one SRO (school resource officer). I encountered four to five security guards standing at each egress and every outside door. I get to the sub lady and find out she's out for the week. I guess no info for me.

There are no clocks in this school. It's like Vegas. No sense of time, just wait for the bells.

Guess I'll go back to the room and wait for the next two hours. I take a seat in the teacher's chair at his desk and peruse the bookshelf behind me. I select *The Big Book of the World's Worst Decisions.* As I'm sitting there, leaning back, my feet on his desk reading his book, the teacher walks in. What?! Apparently, he is doing something on campus, and he wanted to be there when the students get there. This is mildly irritating and disrupting at the same time. I pop up and apologize, but he waves me away. He is a largish, gregarious man who is an ex-Marine and seems a bit militant. He has pictures around the room of Obama, Samuel L. Jackson, and other famous people.

It's always interesting to be in a male teacher's classroom. There are really only two types I've noticed: heavy-handed and worksheet driven, and a big jokester where the kids are loud and underworked. This teacher is all worksheets, boring!

As class starts, the kids mention how social studies is so boring. What? I don't understand how this class can be boring with as much fascinating information there is to learn about! Today he has left five front-and-back worksheets for the kids to complete. Yuck! The classes were decent but funny. It was mostly ninth/tenth graders and very workable.

The last class of the day was called seventh hour. There are only six periods in a regular school day, and I was not aware I would be staying past the final bell. Surprise! Little did I know, this class is mostly for students who did not pass the class the first time around. It is also for kids who want to graduate early or take an elective like band or sports and have to make up hours they lose in a day from that elective's practices. I'm not sure how effective it is to have students retaking a class and accelerated students in one class, but it must have some purpose. As the class began, things went smoothly. There were a lot of athletes, a few band members, and the rest were students who sit and stare but do not complete work.

Suddenly, a kid comes to class late with flaming red, frizzy hair which puffed out about a foot off his head. His beard was equally long and rangy, and he could probably pass for a twenty-five-year-old, but he was a sophomore. He was eccentric in behavior but acted more mature yet immature at the same time. Another boy also walked in late to class, was about six feet tall, large build, with a deep voice and two-inch-thick braided hair, about two feet down the middle of his back. He sauntered into the room very casually and sat down. When I gave him the worksheets, he proceeded to turn to the kid next to him and say, "Hey, I need your paper when you're done."

I said to him, "You know when you cheat, you do not learn. Do not copy off his paper."

He looked right at me and said, "I don't care. I've already been in this class." Wow. He really didn't care ,and you could tell by the look in his eyes, he was going to do whatever he wanted regardless of if I redirected him or not. All I could do was enlist the help of other students to stave off the cheating. Some agreed that they would not share their answers, some simply gave me a blank look. I know I'm just a sub, but that doesn't make me dumb and deaf. I probably only changed the outcome of that one day, but it is all I can do.

High School PE

I accepted this sub job the day before, so I knew I could dress more casually and wear tennis shoes. When I got to the school, the sub coordinator was still out, so I had to figure out where I was to go. PE isn't generally in a classroom, so I had to go find other teachers to get direction. I asked a few students where the gym was and headed that way. The hallways were labyrinthine, and it took me a while to even locate a human.

I happened upon a room, which, coincidentally, was the room the PE teacher I was subbing for had, and asked for help. He directed me to her lesson plans, and I noticed it said I was to start at the pool. Pool? It's February! I guess I remember seeing a pool on the campus the few times I've driven past. He pointed in a direction away from the school and said the girls will be in the locker room. Wow, I guess even in the winter they swim!

After walking through the school, across the student parking lot, and winding my way through, I arrived at the school/city pool. There were city workers all around, and the pool was empty, no water. Hmmm...I still wasn't sure if this was girl's or boy's PE, so I found the girls' locker room and announced myself. Right away the girls set me straight as to who I was subbing for and what I was supposed to be doing. They said they change at the pool and then head back to the main building to the workout room. When I asked why they traipse so far out here just to change, they said there are no locker rooms for them and this is the only option. Wow. I immediately head out the pool gates, back through the parking lot, and back to the main school building. Good thing I didn't wear heels today! By now I had been navigating my way through this assignment for thirty minutes and still didn't know where to go. Good thing I have a logical brain and don't give up easily!

Back in the labyrinthine halls, I found a teacher who was opening what looked like a workout room door. I jumped forward and practically assaulted the poor man. I introduced myself and who I was subbing for and found out I was in the right place. Finally! I stuck there, and this PE coach set up the room for the kids. I offered to help several times, but he just told me no. Another female teacher showed up as the kids started to file in. The class was scheduled to last two hours, so I found a place to sit and watch. These kids were all swim team academy members, and since they did not have a pool now, they worked out vigorously. It was very organized, and the kids worked hard. I again asked if I could help and was told no. I wonder why I am here?

The female PE teacher was very young and explained how she and her husband had moved here from Wisconsin a few months ago. She had blond hair, was trim, fresh-faced, and this was her first teaching job. Her husband was hired at ASU to monitor and regulate the sports requirements as set by Title IX, which states colleges must give equal opportunity in athletics. This bill forces universities to comply with equalizing gender in sports. She and I joked about how unpopular he must be around campus. Many people are unhappy about this bill.

This class came an end without much notice and pomp, and I went back to the pool with all of the boys and girls. Their normal process is to start at the pool, change, go back to the main building, and at the end, return to the pool locker rooms to shower and then back to their classes in the main building. They said it is fine with them because during swim time, they stay there and are comfortable. Although the pool locker rooms are outdated, it is comforting to them. Unfortunately, they waste over ten minutes a day just traveling back and forth.

The rest of my day I am to teach health in the PE area. I head back to the room I started in just as the bell is ringing. The health/PE rooms are all the way in the south end of the huge school, so the kids are all late, and I begin to wonder if I'm in the right place. Suddenly, after the bell, kids wander in like a flood and sit quietly in their seats; creepy. The lesson is a quiz they seem confused about, and a project they must start. Boy, these kids seem lost, and I try to figure it out how to help them. One boy doesn't speak English (I think he was Chinese) and needs help and another is very slow and needs a great deal of prompting. Their assignment is to read the novel *Go Ask Alice*. I haven't read this since I was fourteen, so I pick it up and read. As I am recalling, it is a highly inappropriate storyline with details about a fifteen-year-old runaway girl with drugs, physical and sexual abuse, and rape, in the 1970s. Even I have to put it down because it's making me uncomfortable. These are a good bunch of kids, and I ask them if their parents are aware they are reading this book. They said today was the first day of reading it, and their parents didn't have to sign a permission slip. I cannot believe the actions of this teacher. I poll the room after they've been reading a while, and several kids are getting upset and uncomfortable. I sure hope this teacher is planning a big discussion or involving the parents at some point with this novel. Health class? Oh boy!

High School- Ninth/Tenth Spanish

Before I begin, I have to note that, generally, if I have free time while I'm subbing, I write about past days. This will explain why I get off task or blurt things out. Today I'm subbing in a

Spanish classroom. I will expound more, but this current situation I find myself in the middle of must be noticed.

The teacher I'm subbing for has second period prep (break), so I'm hanging out in the room and writing. Suddenly, the door opens and another teacher comes busting in. He's probably about forty-plus, tall, thin, wild-looking blue eyes, messy, stringy blond hair which looks like it hasn't been trimmed in years. He was clearly hanging on to the '80s, with feathered hair, tattered Converse, and dirty ripped jeans. He is wearing a white undershirt and a blue polyester button-down shirt with one too many buttons unbuttoned. His class has thirteen students and is called Strategies. He is harried and harassed by the kids who are sitting in a scattered fashion about the room. They are all talking to each other as well as the teacher and he's trying to get them quiet. As he tries to teach them and get them quiet, his eyes get wilder and wilder. The kids notice and try to give him advice, but he's rejecting them. Maybe he's on speed? It's just so comical to watch!

In period three there is a boy who walks in slowly, takes forever to get out his work, and is completely unorganized. His backpack looks like a paper bomb exploded. As I brace myself, he finally gets started and begins talking. I do not stop him because he is talking about life and current events. He is so well informed and articulate that I am fascinated. He expounds on things like world affairs and giving his educated opinion and is not biased. I'm impressed!

Period four is the Spanish Four class with studious, advanced seniors. As class begins, I listen to the various conversations and chuckle to myself. Suddenly, a boy from another class comes in leaving a two large pieces of cardboard with Hershey kisses glued to them; one with the shape of an M, the other with the shape of a question mark. These are for his girlfriend, and apparently he's been leaving a letter in each of her classes, and the M is the last letter in the word PROM. She reads the note out loud and squeals yes! This is a "PromPosal," and as he presents her with flowers, the whole class sighs. Cute!

As I begin to take attendance, it appears I've angered a student. He doesn't go by his given name and didn't want others to know. He turns around and yells at the class (I am writing everything down as he's yelling), "Only subs can call me that! Don't even start! I'm getting angry! When I get angry it ruins my day! Don't even think about calling me that! I am already angry because my grade went from eighty-one to eighty-five percent and I need an A! Don't start!"

He sulks for ten minutes, and his friend says, "Get over it!"

He shouts, "NO!" He looks just like Biff from *Back to the Future*, and his anger seems fitting.

I notice how many girls are meek and many boys are more feminine. They have soft voices, dress very neatly, and are clean. I'm not saying boys should be dirty and in ripped clothing, and it's nice to see boys who care about their appearance. They are wearing very tight jeans and tight V-neck tees. Interesting!

As the day wears on, I run into "desperate for attention" kid. As an aside, I spent three years writing this book and got to know many kids along the way. I'm actually typing the book in 2016, and today, one of the students told me this kid's name is Nolan. I won't give a last name, but he and the other students approved the use of his name.

Desperate-for-Attention Kid

This sixteen-year-old boy is in the last class of the day and admitted to being desperate for attention. He is tall, wearing black cargo shorts, black socks, black shoes, and a neon pink tank top. He gets up in the middle of class and announces, "I'm going to do math on the board!" By the way, we are still in Spanish class.

Another student sighs and says, "You do this in every class." It is then I name him Desperate. As he does math on the board, he talks to me. I tell him I am immortalizing him in my book and he says, "Good!" I would describe him as a young Vince Vaughn. He is gregarious, obnoxious, funny, smart, and silly. He circulates the room like a movie star, gracing people with his smile and funny words. He shows interest in others and is well liked. Good for him!

High School, Ninth/Tenth-Grade English and AVID

I didn't know this but this teacher came to work sick and called for a sub at 8:30. I responded to the call and prepared to leave my house. I was scheduled to be there by 10:30, so I got there at 10:20. When I got there, they informed me about the sick teacher waiting for me. What? Why didn't they call me and let me know I needed to come earlier? Poor woman!

I get to the classroom and the teacher is waiting. She tells me how she feels dizzy and is trying to finish up lesson plans for me. I tell her I used to be an English teacher and she should just go. I'll figure it out! I really enjoy this school and especially English. The teacher finally thanks me and leaves.

Her classroom is in the oldest wing of the school, which is about a hundred years old.

It turns out that I showed up just in time for lunch. Great. Seems it's the story of my subbing life. Rush, rush, rush, and wait. I decide to sit at the desk and listen to talk radio, but because this building is so old, the signal is terrible, and it is draining my battery. No big deal because lunch is short. The classroom is covered in posters, knickknacks, notices, and projects, and I cannot find the schedule for the day. What's new?

Times? There is no time schedule anywhere. When does class start? When does it end? Is this ninth grade, tenth grade? I am continually asking the students what time class gets out/starts and it is so frustrating! I look in the binder the school gives me, and the schedule there is outdated (according to the kids). Nothing posted on the wall, nothing!

Bonus: bathroom is close, and I found it right away. Best day!

Period five comes in and are juniors for AVID. AVID is a college prep class where they learn to write higher-level papers and get organized to get into college. Class starts with kids battling to sit next to friends and gets loud. I inform them that I have the seating chart and I better not find out they've moved seats. Surprisingly, they move. Unfortunately, this is not the end of it with one particular group of kids. Once I get them settled, I find out they are to be sitting in groups, and they all move to the seats they were trying to get in, in the first place, which I moved them from. GAH! This particular group seems to all be in the same group, which is awesome (she says sarcastically).

As I check on their progress/work, I hear snickers. Seems I'm very funny and my every step amuses them as I pass by. I don't really care unless they are outwardly rude. I get my revenge when they want to use the bathroom and I make them say, "May I please..." More snickers, although he does parrot it back to me and I allow him to go.

As the kids are working in their groups, I find out from a few students that this project was assigned to them two weeks ago and the final draft is due Wednesday. Each person in the group must write a paragraph (one paragraph in two weeks) to make up a five-paragraph essay and they collaborate on the final draft. Did I mention these were juniors in an AVID class? One paragraph in two weeks? I notice that the one group I was having issue with from the beginning of class is now chatting about their weekend, punching and teasing one another. After observing them for ten minutes in which they accomplish zero work and do not even take papers out of their folders, I approach them. They (four boys and one girl) see me coming and glare at me. I'm sure they're thinking, *You're just the sub, so you better not interfere with us*, but I do.

I ask them what they are working on even though I know exactly what they've been doing. They look at me, laugh, and ignore me. I get a little closer and say, "I've been watching you punch each other and talk about your friends, and I know you have a paper due. Your teacher told me to give you time and it is due Wednesday."

They look at me and the bigger, louder one blurts out, "We are done!". I feign excitement and express how happy I am that they are done and that I'd like to see it. I now hear ummms and ahhhs.

The leader of the group produces a thumb drive and waves it around saying, "It's all on here and we're done!" He then turns away from me back to the others, and they all laugh. I press him further and ask him to give the drive to me. I tell him I'll plug it into the computer and help them edit it. I let them know I will not leave them alone until they show me their work. He struts forward and thrusts the thumb drive toward me. I proceed to plug it in to the computer and find a file, two weeks old with four sentences, indented three times. I ask him what this is supposed to be, and he says, "The essay. It is almost done." Oh, I ask him if he has more somewhere else because this is an unorganized semblance of four sentences. He gets upset and tells me how good this writing is, as I walk away from him back to the group. I give him back the thumb drive and say, "If what I saw on this drive was your best work, it is pathetic. As a group of five eleventh graders who have a five-paragraph essay due in two days, this is not good." They all look at me and begin digging in their backpacks. By now three quarters of the class is over, and they are just now beginning to take it seriously. The ringleader still scoffs at me, but he no longer has his allies. Good! He is obviously dragging them down, and they were allowing it. What does it take to get kids to think on their own? Berating? Humiliation? I dislike getting so harsh, but I am not just going to babysit for the day and let them goof off. Some may say it is not my place to press these kids, but I beg to differ.

This class ends, and the last class comes in with gusto. When I say gusto, I mean loud and obnoxious. Just a little hint to all the parents of school-age children: When the teacher tells you your child is an "active participant" in class or is "spirited," really they're telling you your child is difficult. It's possible your child blurts out in class during a lesson and bothers others. Your child is a "fixer-upper," a.k.a. a mess that aggravates the teacher daily. Take note as here are some catchphrases you might hear so teachers can keep their jobs: he needs to apply more elbow grease, a.k.a. he does nothing in class; she's a "slow starter," a.k.a. has to be asked a million times to get started on her work; he needs a "little help," a.k.a. he is so behind all the others he should have a tutor or be in a special class; he is "special," a.k.a. he needs to be tested for special ed; she has a "unique personality," a.k.a. she is such a noisy know-it-all and never shuts up. There are more and I may mention them in further chapters.

This last class must read articles the teacher left and highlight important points. The kids act bewildered as I give directions and many simply highlight every word. No! I go over it again and again and they act like they've never high-lighted text before. We go over what important points are, and hands go up. What now? Cries come from the peanut gallery that no one has a highlighter. How can this be? The teacher gave this assignment, so they must be prepared for it. Not so. I go through her drawers and find a pile of highlighters, but it is too late. Bedlam ensues as some kids hover over others, bullying them to give up their highlighter. Oh no, this is so bad! I see the weak succumbing to the bullies in this fashion. "Because you didn't protest when I took your belonging, I'm entitled to it." How do they exact revenge or fight back? If the weak stand up and fight, they get in trouble, so are encour-aged to be weak to follow the rules.

I demand the bullies give back what they took as the weak

say, "It's okay," or nothing at all. No way! I encourage them to stand their ground and admonish the takers. I had to get really loud and forceful, but I was able to get them to back off and sit down. After they quiet, I tell them to approach me reasonably and ask nicely ("May I please borrow a high-lighter?"). This entire event took about five minutes, and class resumed. It was very frustrating! I honestly don't know if they returned all of the pens as class went by so fast. Day over!

Junior High

I received the call to sub at 7:30 p.m., Monday night. YES! No five a.m. wake up call. This is something I can handle be-cause I am a bit if a pre-planner. This job is for special edu-cation (which I thought we were all calling resource now). I am to start at 9:30 and end at 3:45. I have some trepidations about special ed classes because, generally, they are physi-cally difficult and mentally taxing. Since I am a stubborn woman and always up for a challenge, I accept. Why not?

I would like to remind the reader that at the time of this sub job, my husband and I share one vehicle. My husband had to go to the post office before I left and returned right at 9:30. Yikes, I'm late! I rush off to the school, which is five mi-nutes from our house. When I got there no one seemed to care about the time and they handed me a folder and keys. It turns out the teacher I'm subbing for is an aide who travels from room to room helping kids out, and his first class starts at 9:55. Phew!

The first class was eighth-grade boys. Boys! Always boys for me! Some of them I met last week in PE, and they re-member me. Cool! The teacher I am helping is a cool, calm woman about my age. She taught kinder and first grade for twenty years but is really loving these eighth-grade boys. We commiserate about teaching boys and being moms of teenagers, and I like her right away. Her class is silent reading and then going to watch *Elf* as this is the week before holiday break, so it seems apropos. Heck, I was surprised to have any jobs this week.

The teacher is furiously trying to enter grades into the online grade system, which is brand new to the district. The kids are funny, and I harken back to when I taught eighth-grade English. They tell their teacher the same things I had heard a few years back: "My book is falling apart, I can't read it." "Can I take an AR test?" Can you? I don't know. May you? Yes! "Can I drink water?" Can you? The best one was, "AR points are due today? What? I'm going to take a test later today for ten points." This from a kid who the teacher says usually only gets three to four points per Quiz because he struggles. She calls him Pinocchio to his face. He is outraged but still laughs.

The next class is lunch, and I sit completely alone at a table while the teachers file in and clump around small tables. The lunchroom is a decent size, but it is all eighth-grade teachers. They tell jokes and talk of a potluck they are planning. I'm okay with it because they don't know me, but if feels a little like high school and I'm the new girl. A few acknowledge me, but overall, I am ignored. I'm an unqualified interloper who, in their minds, does not understand the daily grind of being a contracted teacher. They do not know me, yet as I try to mention how I was a teacher for many years, I am brushed off and disregarded. Whatever.

The next class is math, and I find myself with the same group of boys. I wonder (and shall ask) if this school always segregates boys from girls. This teacher is giving an AIMS pre-test, but she tells the class it is not for a grade. Then she tells them the two classes before them barely scored fifty percent and how bad this is. She passes out a booklet they can write in and a bubble sheet. She plays instrumental Christmas music and displays a roaring fireplace on the projector. The kids are subdued and begin. Some finish and sleep or mill about.

An interesting observation: one class is showing kids' movies and another class is taking a quiz.

Onward to science class where I've been instructed to integrate two other classes in the lab. Upon entering the room, it is mayhem with sixty-six students all mushed together in a largish room. A teacher with a heavy Boston accent hands out a chart where students will fill out results as he litmus tests different liquids. The kids are not involved, and many cannot see what he is doing to even observe, so they are off-task for a bulk of the time. What chaos! When my class is released, it is a relief and more manageable. I take them to the special ed room, where they sit back and read. Ahhh, peace!

Final period of the day is Language Arts, and it is all girls. Wow! There is a girl wearing a Jethro Tull T-shirt and a Rush wristband, wild! The objective is to finish an essay which will be graded as a final exam. When the girls talk during silent reading, the constant threat is, "You better get to work or you will be going to RTC and writing a plan." I'm not sure what any of that means, but the girls laugh and have plenty to say. RTC is never assigned even when she catches a few writing scathing notes on a classroom binder. Sounds like there needs to be better control with consequences, but oh well. This is not my classroom or for me to say.

Eighth-Grade Special Ed

I accepted the sub job especially when I learned it was for the same teacher as before. I'm sure that name sounds familiar. Boston accent? I arrive at the Junior High, check in with the sub coordinator, and find out I will be in an eighth-grade Language Arts class for five days next week. This teacher is so excited to have me as I am a certified, highly qualified Language Arts teacher. I tell her how excited I am because I taught eighth-grade English but am on sabbatical due to having MS. She lets me in on a little secret that another teacher will be out from the end of Spring Break on and asks if I would be interested. Yes! She said she'll let me know after she talks to the principal.

Today I am a Special Ed aide/teacher, so off I go! I head to the Boston accent teacher's room, and Mr. Bob is there. He remembers me from the other time I subbed in that room. The kids start filing in and I notice how shiny and clean they are. It's the week after Christmas break, so the girls have pretty hair, and the boys have new shoes, jackets, and haircuts. The kids are friendly, and when I ask a few questions about them, they smile and are ready with answers.

I am the lead teacher, but the other aide takes over because I'm a sub. I tell her I can do it, but she waves me away saying she is learning to be a teacher. Math is her strong suit, and the kids love listening to her. She is from Michigan and moved here with her family a year ago. She is very frustrated with our school system and wonders why we don't test like they do in Michigan. In Michigan, they begin the year with a few weeks of last year review. They standardize test the students in early October and get results immediately. They then use that information to guide the students for the rest of the year. There is no "teaching to the test" or class time wasted due to weeks and weeks of testing. The pressure is off, and students and teachers can spend the rest of the school year learning, up to the last day before finals. To a teacher, that sounds wonderful and utilizes every minute of the school year.

Currently, we (Arizona) spend the first few weeks doing review, then begin actual on-grade curriculum. Around February we start incorporating AIMS/AzMerit (State Standardized Testing) pre-testing and curriculum built to help kids become successful on the test. We then spend some of March and some of April testing and make-up testing, which halts a teacher's progress because not all kids are in class every day for weeks. This process makes students lose almost a month of actual content and progress toward becoming more proficient at their grade-level. Since the students know the test was over this current year's curriculum, they stop trying and spend April to May barely trying. They do not care, and the teacher's job is made immensely more difficult. Students know the teachers are burned out due to the high-pressure testing, and they are burned out from all the test prep and endless days of learning nothing. It is a lose-lose situation, which could be remedied by simply adopting a different schedule. This doesn't rock the boat much but would be an adjustment.

I know of many parents today who feel standardized testing needs to be gone or greatly diminished. I see the merit in testing but not in the test prep or teaching to the test. So many teachers quit or have their jobs on the line if testing doesn't go as well as the school wants them to. I'll address the persecution of teachers in a later chapter, but this aspect is a giant part.

When the students get working, the other teacher has a million questions for me about being a teacher in AZ, ethics, and grading practices. She has two children in grades six and nine. She laments to me about her son's final grade of 79.94 percent in a "non-core" class. Why didn't they round the grade to an 80 percent? "It ruined his GPA and he lost out on getting a 3.0 by .06 percent," she tells me. She wonders if she should encourage her son to approach the teacher or if she should do it. I tell her that if this is the grade printed on his report card, it is done. She says he got an 80 percent on his final, so his grade must be higher. Unfortunately for she and her son, if he got an 80 percent on the final and a 79 percent in the class, he had a much lower grade before the final. She and I chat as the kids take a math test. I think she'll be a good teacher who stays informed and interested.

Class is over, and it is time for me to head to another room. Today is the day eighth graders are bussed to the high school for orientation to prepare them for ninth grade. My job is to help the ones who are left behind. This next math class is led by a long-term sub who has no teaching experience. This man currently has an inner-ear infection and a bit of a Spanish accent. Oh boy! This other teacher is also helping in this class, and the other substitute is working a problem on an overhead projector. There are about forty kids in the room and are supposed to be copying the problem from the board for greater understanding of the process. Only five or so are copying material down, and most are copying off each other or messing around. When I ask if they need help, many say they don't understand or "get" most of what the sub says.

At this point in the day, the principal came to the room where I was subbing to talk to me about being the long-term substitute for a seventh-grade Language Arts teacher. He and I chuckle when he tells me she is a first-year teacher who is only taking four weeks off when the baby is born. Right! This is her first baby, and his eyes twinkle when he tells me she is young and thinks she'll be back right away. I let him know that is no problem as I have plenty of experience.

As I head back into the room, I notice many teachers use the question-and-answer method and generally call on students who are talking out. This is not the fairest method, as the sane, quiet students do not get called on, even though they raise their hands. Kids who always make noises or blurt out end up getting the majority of the attention. Some who feel embarrassed by life or try to keep their heads down get picked on. It is an old method but ends up leaving out the middle.

I proceed to the science room, where I find a large female teacher who has a two-year-old. Now, her two-year-old is not here in the room, but as much as she talks about him, he may as well be. She sits at her desk in the back of the room with all of the students' desks facing the front toward a projector screen. She asks them (still sitting at her desk) to get out their notebooks as they are going to watch a video and take notes. She tells them the video is "old and boring" but too bad. She played a few minutes of the video and stopped it to ask them questions. Not one single student raised their hand to answer, so she gets louder and asks the same question again. This time one student close to her desk raises her hand to answer. From her desk, this teacher continues the video and instructs them to keep taking notes. The video droned on, and she stops it to shove a paper under the document camera. She tells them to copy the notes into their notebooks. She asks another question, and no one responds. She begins to get frustrated and berates the students for not participating. I keep thinking if she would just get up and walk around, smile, or look into their eyes a bit, they would be participating.

Now she decides to pick on one particularly quiet student who happens to be in my Special Ed group. I had noticed how he's always quiet, almost reclusive but never does any work or bother people. He doesn't want to answer and says he doesn't know the answer. She continues after him (mind you, she still has not gotten up from her desk and the students' backs are facing her) and wouldn't stop until the girl next to him gives him the answer. He mumbles the answer, and she finally gets up out of her chair. She grabs a bag of candy and entices them to give answers. The students perk up and started raising their hands. She resumes the video and notes until the end of class. Although she gave out candy and hands were raised, she still only called on the few close to her desk and she never took more than two steps away from her chair.

My last class was eighth-grade Language Arts, and I came into the room after the bell. I had to use the bathroom, but as I came in, the teacher was yelling at a rowdy room of kids saying, "Come on, guys, read!" She would turn around and make a joke or chat with another student, getting them off task and loud again. This went on for ten minutes before she looked at me and said, "They are always like this."

Another girl close by leaned in and said, "It's like this every day. We never get work done." I laugh and look at the teacher as she nods in agreement.

I say, "Oh isn't that a nice thing to say!" I hope they don't tell others about that. Doesn't make the teacher look very good.

Junior High Eighth Grade Language Arts

This job was offered to me in December as a week-long gig. I happened to be subbing for a special ed teacher who roves from class to class, and this teacher's class was one of those classes. She saw I was proficient in teaching Language Arts and said she was going out of town. Yes! Yes! I love teaching Language Arts! I will sub the heck out of that class!

One of my favorite parts of taking this job is that this teacher had first hour prep, so I don't have to be in class until 9:50 a.m. Very cool! My husband and I go get breakfast burritos, which also becomes my lunch. When I get to the school, I find out the teacher did not go out of town and only needs me Monday through Thursday. Bummer! Her lesson plans are light, and she even says I can do what I want and can even make copies if I want to. Ummm, not cool. Why, oh why, do I talk to people about myself? It only allows people to take advantage of me like this. However, I am a tree, I can bend.

The worksheet ideas she left for the assigned reading stories were complicated and would require much explanation. I go ahead and make up an activity. This is a strategy I discovered in a training class about reading.

Second period is all girls, and many are loud. I establish myself immediately and they quiet down. I have them AR read (Accelerated Reader/silent reading) for twenty minutes as a warm-up. I only tell them to be silent one extra time. I have a no-nonsense approach to teaching, and they seem to respond. After twenty minutes of silent reading, I pass out the white paper, which I instructed them to fold into quadrants. They looked perplexed at first, then laugh when they realize it means quarters or fourths. Teaching Language Arts you must challenge them with language, right?

One of my favorite parts of subbing is this next class and their attitude, walking in the door. The all-girl fifth-period class comes in so proud to tell me that they talk all during AR and are their teacher's most difficult class. I love it when they tell me this because I now know how to handle them instead of working hard to try to figure them out. I smile and tell them their teacher is not here and that behavior will not be happening. As a result, I only had to snap at them a few times and they were silent. I merely repeat, "You WILL be silent while you read," like a mantra. One must just say it firmly and sweetly and the children will comply.

Throughout the day I had one honors class (all boys) and three regular ed classes (two all girls, one all boys). I didn't give the reg ed classes a choice, and we all did the white paper folded into quadrants activity, instead of the worksheet the teacher left. When I offered them a choice, the honors class wanted to do the worksheet left by the teacher. This worksheet was the same for all classes and wasn't particularly an honors-level assignment. As convoluted as this worksheet was, very few of them actually completed it. They fumbled through the story and wrote their answers in incomplete sentences, lacking punctuation, spelling, and grammar. The worksheet was so complicated, it was almost as if it did not allow them to have a thorough thought process, so they just gave up. I decided next time I sub an honor's class, I will not give them a choice on what they want to do. They do not always know best.

We had a good three days, so I tell them I will bring in my *Apples to Apples* game and we will play on Thursday. They are very happy, as I have made them work hard and even graded some of the work they did. I'm a tough grader, and they didn't seem to mind at all. You know, it's funny that when you have higher expectations of a child, they will rise to the occasion. When you lower expectations and only require a minimal level of effort, the children will lower to that and feel it is not worth their time. In any case, their attitudes were wonderful, and we spent Thursday playing our game. This game is all about words and similes, so it fits into the Language Arts paradigm. The kids love it and don't even realize they are learning.

Thursday, every class played *Apples to Apples*, and we had the best time. The kids group up at the tables, and I circulate the room to make sure everyone has a fresh supply of red cards. I love this part because I get to listen in and laugh along with them. They are silly, loud, and working together in groups they may not have picked for themselves. This game forces you to get to know the people in your group, which makes it more than just a word game. It is chaotic, and at the end of the day, I am exhausted but happy.

Tuesday, Junior High Seventh-Grade Language Arts

Today I am shadowing a teacher who is going on maternity

leave. I was approached by the principal months ago and asked if I would consider taking on a long-term sub position. The principal is a small, quirky, older man who runs a tight ship and I respect him greatly. I had only subbed at this junior high a few times before he sought me out. He said he had heard great things about me and would love to have me accept the position. After careful consideration, I decided to accept the job. I've never met this teacher going on leave, but it is seventh-grade Language Arts, which is right up my alley. This teacher only has four weeks of maternity leave. The principal and I have a nice chuckle about young folks being able to bounce back so soon after birth and go back to work. It is her first baby, and we all know she won't want to come back.

Fast forward to today as I begin learning about this position I accepted. I arrive to the school at 9:30 even though the school day starts at 8:25. This teacher has first hour prep, so her day doesn't officially start until 9:55. I head toward her classroom, but since I couldn't remember the room number, I peek into doors in the seventh-grade wing. I wander around for a while and finally find the entire seventh-grade team in room thirteen. I wasn't told we were meeting so am surprised to see all the teachers. We sit for a minute, then she and I head to her room as she starts to tell me about herself. She is a very young first-year teacher and has a very casual attitude about being prepared each day. She laughs about how she goes to an older veteran teacher each morning, to get the day's work. She says it is so easy and that is what I should do as well. Easy? Easy is being pre-prepared, but this is not easy and too on the fly to be a prepared teacher. I suppose if you never want to be creative, think on your own, or use other people then it's easy. I know you're pregnant, but that's no excuse for professional laziness. I know I won't do that and I'll contribute.

Before we open the classroom door for the day the teacher turns to me and says, "Ugh. I can't stand to look at their faces." The bell rings, and kids start gathering outside the door. She opens the door, and the kids start filing in. This is the first day back after a two-week break and they seem a bit spacey. The classroom is clean and sparse, and the kids get quiet right away. She seems to have good control over the kids, so that is a plus.

This teacher is paired with an older teacher who also teaches seventh-grade Language Arts. As we chat before school and during lunch, I learn they have no qualms talking about the kids. For goodness sake, some of these kids are close and can probably hear them. Some examples are "I'm surprised that girl isn't pregnant yet" (may I remind you we are talking about seventh graders?), "See that boy there? His father moved here so he can go to the big high school because he's going to be a star football player. What a joke!" "See that one, two large earrings, gelled hair, and the kid thinks he's God's gift to women. He won't amount to anything because he's dumb as a stone." I could go on and on but that's all I could remember for now.

There is a student who speaks zero English and is given color-by-number coloring pages while the class listens to lecture or does work. He sits bewildered while kids chat and laugh around him. He is taken to a computer and given head-phones where he plays an online game to learn English. I would think he could use a little interaction with the class instead of being isolated away. Kids learn best when forced to assimilate with their own age group. Another kid in class sleeps all period. She says the "office" says it's okay. Hmmm... At one point she goes on and on about a new project but doesn't write anything on the board or give a handout. By the time she is finished giving the kids instructions, I personally have forgotten all the details. I'm a big believer in visual learning, so I lose interest. The project was an essay, and she goes over elements of an essay. Without being specific, she talks about them coming up with a concluding sentence. She breaks grammar rules like, do not start a sentence with a question word unless you are asking a question, do not start a sentence with a number or date, but that never happens. She says she doesn't teach grammar at all. I would begin with grammar rules and transition words before anything and feel like jumping out of my skin. Teaching these impressionable kids improperly can really mess them up for high school.

I'm going to say that, overall, it was a boring day. The first half of class was quiet as the kids read silently for twenty minutes. She then went over classroom procedures and discipline, which is odd because it is the end of March. The last part of every class period she takes the kids to the library where the librarian goes over procedures and talks about popular books. I understand this is necessary, but it was so boring.

(My description of this long-term sub job for seventh-grade Language Arts is going to get bumpy, so I'll tell it to you as I was writing it down. I wasn't able to chronicle every single day but grabbed highlights or frustrations.)

Day Two, Seventh-Grade Language Arts

When I handwrite the summations of my experiences, I often make notes in the margin. In the margin of the following rant, I wrote stars and exclamation points that left dents in the paper. With emphasis I begin!

I have to start the day in the middle. Do we only strive for middle? Why don't teachers hold their jobs and craft in higher regard? I have read the thesis statements of the seventh-grade honors students and am appalled! I have one class a day, which is honors level. I mentioned before that this teacher is instructing them incorrectly. I did a fair bit of research and found out I am right. I mean, possibly in the few years since I quit teaching they have come out with a new method. I've decided to create a visual to project on the screen, so they can see what the difference is. Immediately, I get loud protesting from the packed house. They say, "Our teacher said a thesis is a general statement and you don't want to give it all away." To some extent, this is true but without going into too much detail, I'll say they were doing it wrong for an honors class. Honors is about rigor, and in order to have rigor without extra work, they must raise the quality of their work. I tell them this, and a few calm down. I said it is okay for the regular classes to learn a vague way and then get more specific over the years, but as honor students, they are held to a higher regard. More calm. I tell them they should not be doing the exact same work as the reg ed students; otherwise, why have an honors class? They agree.

<u>Day Six—Seventh-Grade Language Arts</u>

I must re-begin and lay it all on the table. Today is my sixth day of this long-term sub job. From day one, I've had zero lesson plans or even a timeline of topics. There were no copies made, papers graded, or directions given. This school is so darn lucky I used to be a seventh-grade Language Arts teacher, have given AIMS prep assignments, created lesson plans, and can manage a classroom like a pro. For the eighty-five dollars per day I get paid, this is quite a lot of work, and I am less than thrilled. However, I accepted this job and will see it through.

These kids have pushed me from the first minute I stepped in the room, and I've had to push back very hard. I was asked by another seventh-grade teacher how things are going for me, and I say, "Okay." I say it is a good thing I used to teach seventh-grade Language Arts. Their response was, shockingly, "Oh, she gets her plans from another teacher, so you're lucky. She'll do all the work for you. Check with her daily." Truly, if I were the teacher or principal, I'd be embarrassed. The really funny part of this plan is that I DO try to seek out this other teacher every morning and can never find her. I go to her room, to the lounge, other rooms, the copy room...no teacher. If I do find her in time, I cannot get to the copy machine to get ready for the day because she doesn't make the copies for me. This is absolutely ridiculous. Why be dependent on someone else when we are supposed to be trained, educated professionals?

Here are my responsibilities each day. Please remember I am a sub, get no benefits, and am paid (before taxes) eighty-five dollars a day. Every morning I must turn on each computer (five) and password unlock them, write daily lesson plans up on the board (remember, I've been given zero guidelines or plans by the teacher), and track down this other teacher, if I can find her. Since I haven't been able to consistently find her, I've decided I'm done depending on her. I created my own plans based on what I heard she is doing so we have some consistency. I was supposed to have email and gradebook access, but after a week, still nothing. Teachers take attendance online, but I still have to get printed rosters before school and make sure each period of the day I send it back to the office. Then the bell rings for the day to start. At the end of the four weeks, I never gained access to the gradebook or email and had to take attendance every class period, by printed paper from the office.

The second the kids walk into the room it is non-stop activity. Constant questions and problems that need answers and remedies. They look to me with total confidence, which is probably because from the second I stood in front of them as their teacher, no matter how I was feeling, I never wavered in confidence. I took over like I'd been there with them all year, and the students responded. Here's a few of the questions and issues I must remedy each period:

"Can I take an AR test?" ("May I please...)—fifty timesa day

"Can I go to the library?" ("May I please...)—fifty times a day

"Can I move to another seat? I'm cold/hot/can't see/can't hear." ("May I please...)

"Can I go to the nurse/bathroom/get a drink?" ("May I please...)—fifty times a day

"I need help."

"I was absent, can I get the make-up work?" ("May I please…)

"I can't find my essay/homework/worksheet you just handed out/pencil."

"I don't have a pencil/pen/paper"—Is there a question?

"Can I have a pen/pencil/paper?" ("May I please…)

I had originally wanted to write about each day as they happen, but the past week has been a whirlwind of events and drama, so I'll only write about situations as they individually arise.

Period two is all boys, and they are (according to their real teacher) the most difficult class. True to form, they spent our first day together acting terrible. They push, talk out, yell, get out of their seats, take and break other people's pencils/pens, slap books on each other, punch, flick people, and hide each other's things. These are just a few of the daily occurrences in this class.

Day one and two, we (every period of the day) were told to do AIMS writing practice. We reviewed Thinking Maps (graphic organizers) to do pre-writing and began writing the rough copy of a business letter. I personally did a bunch of research to refresh my memory on the format of a business letter. I gave directions, and they acted lost and confused. I repeated directions almost ten times and answered repetitive questions for quite a while. I could see they thought this was a joke and were messing around and not paying attention, so I told them question-and-direction time is over. I told them they need to read the prompt (given to them each) and get started the best they can. Oh man! You would have thought I asked them to put leeches on their eyeballs or chew off their own leg! The cries of protest and whining were cacophonous!

I walked back to the front of the room as they were all screaming at me. I managed to quiet the din and reiterated that I was NOT answering more questions and they needed to use their own brain at this point. I reminded them that during real AIMS testing, the teacher is not allowed to speak to them at all and they have to read directions and do it. They do not care and are still screaming at me. Some are saying, "Why won't you help us?" I forcefully tell them to think for themselves, figure it out, and BE Quiet! I do want You, the reader, to be aware that this happened in every class, which is an indicator of how the teacher has them trained to act.

As I walk back to my desk, they were angrily quiet, and several hands went up. I ignored them and sat down. Just as I got them quiet and working, the principal walked into the room to check on how things are going. The boys erupted in pandemonium, shouting and running to him like angry little toddlers. UGH! They were yelling, "We have questions, and SHE won't help us at all! SHE is refusing to talk to us! SHE is ignoring us! WE don't know how to do the assignment and SHE doesn't care!"

Dr. Anderson went to see what they were working on and noticed it was AIMS practice. He approached me and I immediately tried to defend myself. He stopped me and addressed the class. "SHE is right, and since it is AIMS practice, you need to figure it out."

Instantly, one of the boys yells, "Did you really say we need to cut down all the trees?" Let me elaborate and tell you the letter-writing prompt asked the kids to write a letter to the principal about their thoughts on cutting down all the trees on campus to conserve water.

This boys' outburst caused a whole barrage of questions and shouts from the kids. Wow, the kids are really showing their colors by shouting at the principal of their school. Who do they think they are? If this were my real class, I would never tolerate this behavior. Again, it is clear to me that their real teacher allows this. Dr. Anderson shuts down the shouting by calmly addressing their concerns with facts, and they seem satisfied. On any given day in my time as their long-term sub, they behaved poorly, and every day was a battle of wills. I'm not sure I agree with having all of the same sex in one room. The girl classes are whiny and manipulating, and the boy classes are loud and violent.

In this same second-period class, one boy starts trouble frequently. His name is spelled incorrectly on the attendance roster, and when I forget and mispronounce his name, it creates an uproar of laughter and jeers by the other boys. It always takes a few minutes to get them calm again, so I can continue to take attendance. I have a headache almost every day after second period and think, *Why am I torturing myself with this job? I committed to it, but, man, I do not want to fight with these boys every day!* From the first day I am their sub, this boy is squirrely and blurts things out. Their real teacher had warned me about this, and I scold him frequently. He seems to expect the scolding, and she has him sitting in the very back of the room, away from the other kids. As the period progresses, I find things to praise him on, and he starts to smile. The next day he's a little better and I allow him to take the attendance to the office. The other boys tell me I'm making a huge mistake, but I tell them not to worry about him. He smiles at me and leaves the room. Of course I am secretly praying he doesn't mess around out there and does what he's told because I don't want to look like a fool. He returns in a few minutes and quietly sits down. I nod to him, and he smiles again. Success! Now let's not fool ourselves and think he's cured. He's not but his transgressions are fewer and fewer by day.

On the second Friday I am his teacher, he approaches me to ask questions about molestation. He said he hears a lot about it on TV shows but can't ask his dad because he works a lot. He asked if I minded telling him. I don't mind and begin to tell him in a very PG version. I know if my son asked his teacher because he couldn't ask me, I'd want them to be as honest as they can with him. Teachers are parents for the day, and these kids tell us EVERYTHING! Especially a sub because they think they'll never see us again! I tell him about being touched when and where you do not want to be. He says, "You mean in the private part?" I say yes, that too, but it can also mean being attacked when you didn't expect it. The Spanish word is *molestar*, meaning to be messed with in any way you do not want; even vandalism. The student nods and says he understands and says thank you. I allowed this class to play *Apples to Apples* this Friday as a reward for good behavior. They were so excited! We all laughed and joked even though two of the boys wrestled and tried to choke each other. All was good, and I learned a lot about these rowdy boys!

Sadly, their teacher really set these boys in a bad light, but they can be pretty cool. They are boys! They need more attention and positive feedback. Since I have raised only boys, I am more comfortable with the strict line I must hold with them.

One of the classes during the day is **Honors**. I have been hearing other seventh-grade language arts teachers describe these kids. She said, "These kids are so low that Honors is on grade level, regular classes are below grade level, and the low classes are so dumb, you can't do anything with them." I am horrified to hear this! How can these teachers lump all these self-imposed stereotypes into one mass class of seventh graders here, and is that giving up? There are about four hundred seventh graders here, and we are just giving up? She says, "This year of seventh graders are awful!" I can understand a few but ALL?

The first day of me taking over, I notice the assignment board is separated into two sections: "honors" and "on level" The on-level classes have detailed descriptions with CW (classwork) and HW (homework). The honors assignments simply say, "SAME," with an arrow pointing to on level. I decide that when the honors kids come in, I'm going to talk to them about it. As tough as I am, I am a big proponent of allowing the kids some say in their education. I don't always take their advice, but it creates a sense of ownership in them, and they generally rise to the challenge.

I speak with them and immediately let them know that their agenda plans will be different. I explain how an honors class doesn't mean more work, just a higher quality of work with more rigor in the grading practices. They ask what rigor is, and I explain how it is more intense or thoughtful work. I let them know I will expect more quality from them. I expect quality from each student, but from an honors class, it's higher. They seem to agree and understand that their class so far has been a joke. Many of these kids have high aspirations, and their intelligence is being stifled. On we go!

Unfortunately, there are a few students in honors class who refuse to do high quality work, if any work at all. There was one student in particular who was combative with me, daily. I would give directions, go over the assignment, and leave them alone to get started, but his hand would immediately go up. Initially, I would address him and attempt to answer his questions. However, when his question was about the directions already given, I would reply, "I already went over that. Possibly someone else can help explain it to you better." He would get angry and argue with me loudly, saying he has a *right* to get help. He would shout that I am supposed to help him as much as he wants me to and he has a *right*. He would get so combative that other students would tell him to hush, but he refused.

BEHAVIOR of STUDENT

One particular day I handed out the weekly vocabulary quiz, and his hand went up. I simply said, "It is a quiz and directions are on the paper."

He shouted, "You have to help me!" It is worth mentioning he has consistently "forgotten" his homework or essays he was to complete and was currently getting an F. This is probably why he didn't want to do the quiz, because he didn't do his homework. Frustrating, but nothing I can help with. On this day he chose to really get vocal while other students were silent and working on their quiz, so I asked him to go to the office. I was calm, but he was apoplectic! He was waving his arms, popping up and down in his seat, and screaming at me. I called the office, and the principal came down to get him. Sometimes we tend to forget that a teacher has to deal with much more than simply educating your child. Teachers can tell when there is no discipline in the home and the child is spoiled or entitled. When your child is sent to school and acts in this manner, other students lose chunks of learning because of your child. Your child loses as well, but most parents of these kids are too focused on what their child is entitled to have, which sadly is not education but the teacher's energy and time. Time which could be better spent teaching knowledge and getting the kids excited about learning.

The principal did come and take him to the office. He also spoke to me after school that day and updated me on this student. He said he called the father, and the father was upset his son acted that way. The principal said the school has had behavior issues with this child in the past and he's going to put him on a behavior contract, again. I tell him I will do what I can but if he is disruptive to the whole class, I cannot have him in class. There are thirty-two students in the class, and he interrupts their learning. The next day, this student comes to me to apologize, and things are really good for a few days. He does act out several more times before my time there was up, but he was much better.

GRADES

I know I haven't mentioned this teacher's grading policy, but the honors students were particularly upset by it. She feels in order to make things fair and equal for all students, she grades on a ninety-five percent scale, not one hundred percent. Essentially, the A+ does not exist, and if you miss two out of twenty on a quiz or assignment, it is a B. On a one hundred percent scale, it is a ninety percent, or A-. When I told the students in the honors class, so many of them realized that no matter how hard they work, it is almost impossible to pull an A- in this class. Most kids had B's or C's and were trying for A's. When we re-calculated their grades based on a one hundred percent scale, they were greatly improved. From then until the end of my four weeks with them, I had two columns for their grades, and they took comfort in that. Their relief in knowing their hard work can pay off was palpable.

It is often defeating to a student who strives higher and higher, possibly for perfection, to know no matter what they do, they will never reach a hundred percent. I proceeded to ask around the teacher's lounge to see if anyone else was doing that, and not one teacher was. One teacher mentioned how the staff talked of it, but it was never implemented. Wow, did I open a can of worms! As well, the school policy is NO zeroes. Again, with this fair and equal garbage. A child who does zero work will at least be assigned a fifty percent. A child who struggles and tries but still gets F's get an automatic fifty-five percent. Some of the kids knew this, but others who struggle were mad. Fifty percent/fifty-five percent is still a failing grade, so the kid who does no work and the kid who does some work still fail. This makes them not want to try at all. In the four weeks I was the long-term sub, I never had access to add grades and only had email the last week. Parents were so upset that there weren't any grades posted in four weeks and were calling constantly. Thankfully, I didn't have to take any flack. I'll tell you, it was a mess!

Standardized Testing Day—Junior High

I am still deep in this four-week, long-term sub job.

I have administered these tests for years as a regular, contracted teacher, but as a sub, I need to follow the lead of the certified teacher assigned to be in the room with me.

I arrive to school just before eight a.m. and head to my room. I know I have to cover posters in my room, and kids will be filing in at 8:33 a.m. I have been given a huge roll of butcher paper, which I cut and staple over the various posters that give educational words of advice. Wow, what a frustrating task! In years past I would either remove the posters or cover them with white copy paper, but I do what they want. I set about my task and realize I have no idea if I'm picking up my tests or if the partner teacher I've been assigned will do it. I had attended the staff AIMS meeting, signed a confidentiality form, and they gave me an instruction booklet so…I figured I was it. Oh, not so! This is so confusing, and as I've said before, they (the school admin) are so lucky I've administered these tests to seventh graders previously. Ugh! Such a game of cat and mouse or "button button, whose got the button?" I'm pretty sure I'm the only long-term sub on campus, so how about give me info!

Fine! I head to the lounge to drop my lunch in the fridge, get mail from her box, and decide to swing by the library where the test boxes are being handed out. There are cookies! Uck! Cookies for the teachers for breakfast? I don't mean to be sour or ungrateful but come on! We need fruit, juice, bagels, or even muffins, not sugary cookies so we crash in an hour. Of course, I take two cookies and hightail it out of there!

LOL! I didn't have time to eat breakfast, and now have a stomachache. We then ask ourselves (again), why are most teachers fat?

When I return to the room, a female teacher is in there with the box of tests, trying to figure things out. I've never met this woman before, but I know she is the Spanish teacher. She is forty-six years old, wearing a stretched-out brown sweater with a large fox stitched on it. She is wearing a pair of loose grey yoga pants and thong sandals. Her hair has about three inches of grey dark roots with the rest bleached blond. Her hair is fashioned into two pigtail braids, with a rubber headband. Her clothes are extremely wrinkled and seem to be quite old. She looks at me like she wants to know how to administer these tests with wide, questioning eyes. When I try to tell her how we should proceed, she scoffs and does it her way. Okay, then.

As an aside, she is standing next to me while I write all of this in my spiral notebook and is clueless.

The AIMS test directions are very clear, and the school provides pencils to give to the kids. Unfortunately, she does not follow directions or my guidance, and things become chaotic. A young counselor pops into the room to see if we need help and sees the chaos. I try to convey that I'm frustrated, but she misses my hints. This female teacher is ignoring me and calling girls up to the desk to sign the attendance sheet while handing them a test booklet. NOOOOOOOO! I try to tell her we are to hand out all materials, make all students stay in their seats, and give directions as one, but she won't hear it. Basically, what is happening is this: some kids have test booklets and answer documents, some do not, and

ALLLL kids are talking. It's at this point she informs me she did NOT attend the instructional test meeting and seems okay with it. Huh, I kind of figured that out. I am so frustrated I have to walk away because I'm starting to twitch. The young counselor woman is still in the room smiling and pretending everything is okay. I feel like morons surround me!

When I am calm enough to venture back toward the chaos, I see she is now asking if anyone wants or needs a pencil. Of course they do! We have a pile and are required to give them a brand new one! I've been telling them for days that we will furnish them all a pencil so they don't have to worry. I attempt to tell her that the pencils are for the kids, and she completely ignores me. As the girls come forward (mind you, they have a test booklet and answer sheet on their desk now), she reminds them of her rules for borrowing a pencil. She yells, "Remember MY rules! AR book, bling, ID card, or ring (cell phone)!" The girls sigh and begin to take off their earrings, necklaces, get out ID cards, or go get their book. No! No! No! I feel my blood pressure rise, but I must stay silent. My new mantra for sanity is, "I'm the sub, I'm only the sub." I've given this test every year for the past seven years, and watching this woman hack the process to pieces is just killing me. We (the state/school) want the kids to be relaxed, we want them to stay in their seats reading quietly until we begin. Once again, I must walk to the other side of the room and face the wall. This is insanity!

AIMS is a standardized timed test, and we are on a tight schedule to get the kids done and off to lunch on time. It is now 9:00 a.m., and we have not begun to test. Patience gone, I must but in and say, "We need to speed this up, so I'm handing out the rest of the tests and pencils. You can call them up to sign the attendance sheet." She mildly relents, but I can tell she doesn't like me as she feels this is her show. At long last things begin to roll along smoothly and the girls are all quietly in their seats.

This teacher opens the teacher guide and begins reading the scripted directions, which I had to show her. Seriously? Doesn't the school principal know this person is totally incompetent and has zero idea what she is doing? Apparently not. These scripted instructions are very clear and concise, yet she feels it is necessary to paraphrase and elaborate. There is a script so each class in each school, across the state, are given equal opportunity and the results are valid. Sorry but she is a complete moron. I would love to shout and rip the booklet from her hands, but I remain calm and repeat my mantra in my head, "Just a sub, I'm the sub. Just the sub..." She is openly violating the rules of AIMS test administering and all I can do is write about it. If I tell on her, I'll look like a fool and be mocked because I'm a sub. I stay silent in word but mighty of pen.

The following three-hour testing time goes rather smoothly after we got started, but I know the tests were compromised. Alas, another day where I'm only a substitute. I'm not the real teacher and hold no credibility. Their loss.

Day 2—AIMS

I'll admit I truly did not have intentions to write about this process every day. However, I am spurred on by my observations.

Before school, I was walking toward the office, when I saw

the female teacher I was paired with yesterday. She and her husband were just walking onto campus. She looked right at me and looked the other way. I continue toward them, make eye contact, and say, "Good morning." She looks uncomfortably at me and mumbles, "Uh, hi." Are you kidding? We spent over three hours together yesterday and she doesn't remember me? Wow. I continue on to the office and decide I do not care.

When I return to the classroom, she is sitting there. Yesterday when I mentioned she was thin, I was wrong. I do not mean to be catty, but I am trying to build a mental image for the reader. She is decidedly lumpy. Poochy tummy, saggy rear end, and her clothes make her look worse. Today's sad sweater is the same as yesterday, only grey with an owl stitched on it. She is wearing black, saggy yoga pants, which are too big for her, and a knee-length cowl neck cardigan sweater with cap sleeves to round out the ensemble. The sweater is a large stitch with many pulls in it and has seen better days. Today's shoe to go with the sweater over a sweater look is...drum roll...thong sandals! Her hair is in a ponytail, with the same rubber headband as yesterday. I know teachers aren't generally fashion plates but we could try a little!

*There was a time where teachers were revered, dressed respectfully, acted with authority, and never divulged intimate details about their lives to the students. There was an air of mystery about a teacher, which caused the students to remain in awe and therefore obey. Today, too many teachers try to be the students' buddy, regaling their antics of the weekend or private life to the students of all ages. Some teachers speak in casual parlance or even have the students call them by their first names, high fiving and commiserating with them about boyfriends/girlfriends, breakups and issues with their parents or home life. Today, too many teachers dress poorly, wearing sweatpants, yoga pants, flip flops, T-shirts, jeans and cargo shorts; hair in a ponytail, messy, greasy, or otherwise unkempt. There is an air of casualness which conveys a relaxed atmosphere that students of all ages sense and feed off of. Far too many students know intimate details about their teachers and feel they can be rude or talk out of turn with little to no consequences, as they do in the home. We ask ourselves, why is education in America getting worse? Why are our students in America falling way below the bar in grade level achievement and sliding further down? Why do we shove students through the system with more care for their home life than their academic progress? I will ask the reader to ponder as they read on.

She begins the day exactly as before even though I tried talking to her before the bell rang. I told her the pencils are for the students to have and they do not need to trade a valuable to get one. She nodded like she understood, but when we began, she did the same as yesterday. She again yells, "AR book, bling, ID or ring!" I'm not sure what is wrong with this woman but she is like a robot. I was dumbfounded and had to walk to the other side of the room so I wouldn't say something regretful to her. As I walk about one girl whispers to another, "I don't have anything to trade for a pencil. What should I do?" I lean in and tell her not to worry and I will get her a pencil. I wander over to the pencils, grab a handful under the guise that I am going to sharpen them, and give the girl one. She is visibly relieved and smiles. I am horrified these kids have to feel persecuted to get a writing instrument to take a standardized test!

I now knew I must speak out. I went ahead and emailed the principal earlier in the morning asking to speak with him. I do feel he should know what is going on, and he said he only has a few minutes to talk. Even though I had several things I had wanted to discuss with him, I pick my battles and tell him about this AIMS testing.

The principal is a fast, intense, receptive man who graciously listens to me. Before I can get much further, he pulls in the assistant principal and says, "She knows everything there is to know about AIMS testing." I clue them in to my observations and level of discomfort. Mr. Anderson listens openly as I make it clear I am not wanting to make waves but need them to know. He nods and says he will take care of it. As I previously stated, he only has a few minutes, and as he hurried me out of his office, I feared I had made a mistake coming out with the truth. I got the vibe they were not happy. The day proceeds as usual, and nothing changes. It is out of my hands, and now I must deal with students who have been testing all morning and do not want to do anything for the rest of the day.

Day 3—Wednesday

I get to school early and head to the room. I brace myself for a war because I tattled on this woman and now I have to spend three hours with her. However, as I open the door she approaches me and says happily, "You'll have a new partner today! They are giving me back time in my room and I'll be relieving teachers for breaks. I'm elated!" Clever! Instead of setting her straight, they acted like they were rewarding her with a break. I wonder who will be my partner, but at least I'll be away from this train wreck.

A few minutes later another teacher with a box of AIMS tests comes in the room. She is the culinary arts teacher and immediately humbles herself, letting me know she knows nothing about this process. I set her mind at ease and fill her in on my experience, to which she smiles and says great! Suddenly, female teacher from the past two days pops her head into the room and asks if we need any help. She feels she is now the expert and comes barreling in to take over. I run over and tell her we are great and she does not have to worry. She ignores me and gives Ellen advice on how to hand out the tests and the pencil procedure. I intervene and say, no, we are fabulous, and she should go enjoy her day. Finally, she exits the room and I sigh with relief.

The culinary arts teacher turns out to be a friendly, open person who is about fifty-plus years old. She knows a lot of the students, and they like her. We start chatting about the job, and she asks how I like this sub job. I mention how it is fine, but I was not given lesson plans or directions. I've taught seventh grade before and am managing. I mention how the gal I'm subbing for is cold to everyone. No big surprise but I'm committed to this job and will see it through. The testing goes very smooth, and we get along fine. We did NOT require the kids to give up a personal item for a pencil, and it was a great day.

It is now my last week of this long-term sub job, and the

teacher is due to return after having her baby. The unit I'm told we need to be finishing is poetry, and I am to take all of the classes to the computer lab to complete a poetry notebook. They are to construct poems based on different types of models, using clip art photos. I have been taking them to the computer lab, class by class, for the past few days, and things have been going all right. The students know my time is almost over and I am losing power. Behavior begins to deteriorate, and I must fight harder and harder each day to keep their attention and make sure they are being productive. Each class has their own problems, as two of them are all boys, two of them are all girls, and one is mixed gender honors. The girls become squirrely, talking a lot, trying to get out of doing things by whining or claiming female issues. The boys become combative, throwing things, destroying property, cursing, and laughing out loud when the room is silent.

On the last day of this job, their poem notebooks are due, and we are all in the computer lab. Some students are done and goofing around, others are crying about how they haven't been given enough time and feel cheated. I tell them their regular teacher will be back Monday, and SHE will be grading these, so they better work hard. More whining and excuse-making throughout the day make it impossible to look upon them fondly as I end my time with them. I had been having issues with one of the all-boy classes (as previously mentioned), where they were calling me "girl" and "woman" thinking it was funny and going into hysterics when I reacted. I had been deep breathing, telling myself this is almost done and you never have to see these kids ever again, but it is increasingly difficult.

This last day we are in the lab as I stated. I look over to see a group of boys digging into their backpacks and snickering. I walk over and see they are not halfway done with their poem notebooks, and one boy has a bag of Cheetos he has opened. The computer lab rules specifically state No Food or Drink, so I tell him to put the food away. He looks at me with a gleam in his eye and whines, "But I'm hungry!"

I walk away as I know the longer I engage, there will be a battle of wills, and I wish to get out of this job unscathed. I sit down at the teacher desk in the room and know he has not put the food away but is now sharing it with others around him. I stand up and say, "I asked you to put the food away and need you to do that, right now."

The boy loses his mind and says, "I don't have any food and don't know what you're talking about! GIRL, you crazy!"

That is it. I cannot take it another second and I grab the edge of the table next to the desk with both hands saying, "What did you just call me?!" I walk around the desk and quickly approach him as he rapidly shoves the bag of Cheetos back into his bag.

"I don't have anything! I don't have food!"

I lean in close as I work to regain my composure and say, "Go to RTC (their version of a detention/discipline program) right now and I will send the form with another student."

He looks at me with large eyes, acting like I'm crazy, and jumps up from his chair. He yells, "You crazy woman!" grabs his bag, laughs out loud, and walks out of the room. The rest of the students are totally silent, and when I look at them, they turn and quickly get typing. I've had smaller run-ins with this boy throughout the four weeks, but we were always able to resolve things in the hall or quietly beside his desk. I see him as a young man with great potential to be a leader. I have told him so, to which he seemed to understand. At this point in our teacher/student relationship, I feel I have made zero progress with him and hang my head in shame. He is ONE of 150 students I have every day, and my largest regret is that I could not reach him.

As that class draws to a close, along with the others, and my four weeks comes to an end, there is a knock on the classroom door. Every Friday at this school, the last forty-five minutes of the day is a time where kids who haven't completed homework throughout the week can sit in a classroom and get caught up. If they have completed their work for the week, they get to go outside and play volleyball, tetherball, buy ice cream, or just socialize with their friends. I'm sitting in the classroom with about five other students working when he knocks. I go to the door, and standing there is the boy whom I've had problems with these four weeks.

This is the same boy I sent to RTC today and feel defeated about. He comes to me with paper in hand, asking me to sign that he has talked to me. This releases him back to class (whichever his last hour class is) from the detention room. I ask him if he understands why I sent him out of the room. He says yes and that he is sorry. No one is around us, and he doesn't have to show off or posture. I tell him I am sorry I lost my cool and yelled at him, and he says he understands. I say, "Do you understand why you upset me more than the others who misbehave?" He nods but I continue. "You are a boy that others look to for guidance. I see people in the class watching you. You have all the makings of a confident leader, but you must choose to behave in a more mature manner. I know you are only in seventh grade, but maturity comes as you age, and I would just like to let you know I really think you are important." He looked at me with wide eyes and nodded okay. It seemed to me that he was paying attention, but I have talked to him before and here we are. Maybe he will think about what I've said and our four weeks together, but maybe not. It is quite possible I was the mouse and he was the cat, and at night, he smiles and laughs at the game. I hope not.

As an aside, four years later I was subbing at the local high school and he was in one of the classes, along with a few of the other kids from the honors class and such. He recognized me before I recognized him. This was an eleventh-grade English class, and he sat in the back. One of the girls who had been in the honors class came to talk, as she also recognized me. Before I took attendance, this young man yelled out, "Mrs. Hill! Are you the teacher who taught our seventh-grade class while our teacher had a baby?" I said yes, and he came up to talk to me. He calmly asked how I was and if I still like subbing. We had a nice conversation and he smiled and said, "Well, it's good to see you!"

The girl who had been chatting with me turned to me, after he walked away and said, "He's really changed. He has a job and a girlfriend and he's really nice to be around." I smiled, but I know this girl doesn't know about he and my history from four years ago. She doesn't know about our talk and how I had hoped he would mature and become a good person and leader. I feel so proud of him and decide maybe I can make a difference as a simple, lowly, sub. I'm awfully conceited to think it was me, but who cares?!

Life Connections and Careers—Junior High

I am only a few days out from being a long-term sub here. I am still wondering if I even want to sub anymore this year. Fortunately, I got a call from the teacher who completed AIMS testing with me only months before. I really liked her and am willing to do this for her.

ASIDE: On my last day as a long-term sub here, I sent out an email with my personal information telling them to use me as a sub the rest of this year and next as well. I went into the lunchroom that afternoon, and so many teachers expressed interest. One teacher exclaimed how she'll be out the ninth and tenth, and I can sub for her. I said great, just call it in. She never called in for me nor did anyone else the rest of that year.

Even though I'd been at this school for over a month, it seems no one gives a care to have an experienced teacher sub for them. All of the years I have been subbing in this school district, I have only been requested as a sub, five times. It is baffling to me.

Boys' PE, wrestling, and computer—High School

When I accepted this job, the title was Industrial Arts. I figured it would be woodshop but walked into a classroom filled with computers. I had to do a double-take and check my roster again. Yes, I was in the correct room. This is not the first time the title given on the computer did not match the actual assignment, and being a substitute, I have learned to be flexible. The teacher is in the room and tells me I will be showing movies all day and walks me over to the adjoining theater. This was a very cool theater with a touch screen controlling the screens and audio and theater seats.

He sweeps out of the room as his wrestling team is waiting in the hall for him so they can get on the bus. After he leaves, I notice a man walking around the room. I figured he was another teacher because he wasn't sitting in a chair in front of a computer. He was wearing a brown corduroy jacket, brown leather shoes, and maroon corduroy pants. He has a seriously receding hairline and seems very serious. When I address the students to begin our day, he answers to his name when I call attendance. Whoa! He's a student! I tell him to sit down so we can continue.

The students are good throughout attendance, and we file into the theater. The movie is, *The Treasure of Sierra Madre*, which is Humphrey Bogart. I think to myself, *Ah no! An old black-and-white movie and a dark, comfy theater make for a bad combination in a high school.* Little did I know but this class had started watching it the day before and were very into the movie. Thank goodness! It is a good movie, and I get into it right away. Much of the movie is in Spanish and there are no subtitles, but the kids don't seem to mind.

As soon as that class ends, I run down the corridor to the girls' bathroom. After two hours and a carafe of coffee, I cannot wait. Thankfully, I spotted a bathroom on my way in because that has been a problem in the past. Who knows where the bathrooms are? When I return, the next class is waiting for me in the hall, and I let them in.

This class is watching *12 Angry Men*, which is another black-and-white film with Ed Begley Sr. and Henry Fonda, among other great actors of that time. The entire movie takes place in a jury room after a trial, and they have to decide on a final verdict. It has great cinematography and acting, but it is a bit boring with great, long pauses for effect. Unfortunately for this class, they aren't getting into it, and I have to keep shushing them. One girl keeps saying, "I don't watch black-and-white movies!" over and over. Tough! This is school, and obviously, the teacher has a reason for showing it. It is a media class, after all. Another kid argues with everything I say and then exclaims loudly how he annoys everybody. Really, I hadn't noticed!

ASIDE: Something which has annoyed me about this school is how spread out it is. The campus is very large and the distance between the parking lot, classrooms, and office are immense. As well, the buildings aren't marked, and the numbering scheme on the classrooms doesn't make any sense. The hallways are very long and twisty, with little to no direction, and there are staircases everywhere. I have to allow ten to twenty minutes extra in my morning, just for this part of my day. I definitely get a workout in when I substitute teach here.

On day two of this job, I realize this teacher is not only the varsity wrestling coach but also has a first period wrestling class. The first day I was in his class, it was a block day and he only has media classes. Today is regular schedule; no block, and his schedule is very full. He is in the room again when I get there and tells me he is leaving for the weekend for a wrestling meet. He directs me to follow him so he can show me where I need to be when the bell rings. Hmm, very confusing, but I go along for the ride. We head outside and to the gym where we enter the wrestling room. I guess I forgot wrestling is all boys, but I was quickly reminded as there were thirty boys in all states of undress. Many were running and jumping, with only their underwear on! They didn't notice me at first, and I stood in the corner waiting while the teacher/head coach talked to the assistant coach. The boys began running back to the locker room to grab shorts as they were mildly embarrassed to see me in the gym.

I continued waiting uncomfortably while the coach then talked to the wrestlers, yelling and screaming obscenities at them. The boys didn't mind and were getting pumped up. One or two of the boys had to admit they didn't go to practice last week, and he made them do one hundred push-ups, right there. When the coach's back was turned, the boys flipped him off or made rude gestures. I wonder if that happens in all sports or just here with this coach?

Finally, the teacher/coach walks me back to the classroom and says I do not have to go back to the gym today. Phew! I could certainly handle those boys, but if I don't have to, all the better. This teacher has an odd schedule and runs around the campus, all day. After a while, the second-period students come filing into the room, and it is "Computers and Media." Once I get class started, they all decide they do not want to watch the movie he left for them but would rather mess around on their computers. No matter to me and the class moves along smoothly.

The next class is freshman boys' PE and I have to run to get to the gym before the bell. I was told the boys would line up outside the building in ABC order, so I could take attendance, then they would dress out. HA! What a joke. Thankfully, I know how to handle boys and start yelling like a drill sergeant. I had a few of these boys the previous year at the junior high, so they try to act all friendly, but I will not have it. I told them all if they are not in ABC order as their teacher told me they were supposed to be and I call their name as I walk down the line and they are not in the right spot, I will mark them tardy. Not absent because that holds greater consequences with the attendance office.

I start at the front of the line and move down, one by one, softly saying their names. If they weren't right in front of me to say, "here," then I marked them tardy. Boy, you should have been there to hear the whining and complaining as I said, "Ben? Nothing? Okay, then you are absent or tardy." They ran to me yelling, "I am here, I am here! Man, this isn't fair!" When I got to about letter D in the alphabetical names, the boys started realigning themselves. One kid ditched and ran, which is nothing I can help. If I got to the proper kid in the right place in line, I allowed them to leave to go to the locker room early. They loved that! I stayed firm in light of all the whining and crying and peeled them off, one by one.

Now that attendance was done and they were all in the locker room, I waited in the hall outside the door. I know it doesn't take more than a few minutes to get dressed, and it had been over five minutes. I could hear yelling and screaming in there, so I cracked open the locker room door and yelled, "Time's up!" A few came stumbling out, but most stayed in there, playing. I yelled again that I'm coming in un-less they all come out now, and suddenly, they came spilling out of the door. They had their backpacks on and most not dressed out. I took them into the gym and, drill sergeant style, told them to line up again in ABC order that we were doing attendance again.

As they whined, I began and whoever was in line and dressed out, I sent off to play basketball. I questioned each one who was not dressed, and when they gave a lame excuse, I did not let them play basketball. They got to sit in the corner or have a second chance to go get dressed. Most chose to get dressed. These were the biggest bunch of whiners and even complained about having to play basketball instead of field hockey or whatever it was their teacher was doing with them when he is here.

Finally, it was time to stop the basketball games and send them back into the locker rooms to get dressed. Little did I know I would have to babysit them on this as well. Suddenly, a couple of boys came to tell me that the rest of the boys had locked the locker room door and they couldn't get in to get dressed. By this time I was frustrated and furious, walked over to the locked door, and kicked it very hard. The wall shook, and a custodian came popping out of his office nearby. He looked at me with a quizzical look as the boys unlocked the door. I left the custodian behind as I went charging to-ward the locker room door, only to find they were goofing off, laughing, and NOT getting dressed out. I did not go all the way in but shouted through the opening that they better be getting dressed and quit messing around. I then realized there was only a minute of class left, and I needed to be in the next building for the next class. As I was walk/running away from the locker room (all boys still inside being loud), I saw a male PE coach heading in. I nodded at him and began to run to my next class.

ASIDE: I am aware these students take advantage of subs, and every job is a battle. I'm never very surprised when the students don't do the assigned work or act poorly, but it certainly challenges a substitute's nerves. I had hoped to slowly change students mind and attitudes regarding subs, but it doesn't seem promising.

After this most recent experience, I am reminded of why I do not teach anymore. It wasn't necessarily the students but what the administration does to the teachers. This teacher runs around like a crazy man teaching three different preps (teacher speak meaning different subjects to prepare for), just so he can have a full-time job. He coaches the varsity wrestling team and has to prepare for substitutes so he can attend meets or travel out of town. Talking with him, I had the feeling that he would rather be teaching wrestling full time as he seems to love it. His son is attending Harvard on a wrestling scholarship and laments to me that he misses most of his son's matches because he has his own team. He let me know his son has a match in Las Vegas, Nevada (a sister state to Arizona), this weekend and he'd love to miss this school's match and go to his son's. He says it's rare for his son's team to have matches so close to Arizona. He's clearly torn.

He is a good teacher and excellent coach, but he's still a father. Although being a teacher is great when your kids are small, they get older and more involved in activities, and as teachers, we have to miss that. Coaching means more money on the paycheck above the regular teaching contract, but at what cost to our personal children?

OVERBURDENING

I was on a governor's panel of teachers and administrators to help our newly elected Governor of Arizona understand the education system and its flaws. I sat in the room with seven educators, most of whom were principals or vice principals. I was one of the only teachers but was valuable because of my years and varied experience. I had spoken to the governor before when he was running for office, and he knew my stance on education in Arizona. We were all on couches and cushioned chairs in a horseshoe shape, with the governor in the center of the bend. He sat me right next to him, and the cameras were rolling.

Several questions were pre-planned for the governor to ask, but few were for me. I was the foil, I suppose, because after someone answered a question, he would turn to me for a response. One particular question was about teacher involvement in the schools. How much are teachers involved with the students, beyond the regular contract hours? One younger principal of a local charter school answered the question, "We are very proud of our teachers' involvement with the students. Many of our teachers come in before school and assist the students with their breakfast. Many of them have students in their room during lunch or help in the cafeteria. Many teachers stay after school and help with tutoring or after school programs or sports. Many teachers come here on the weekends and coach sports teams." He was very smug and looked at us all like he should be getting the Nobel Peace Prize.

Knowing I would have a response, the governor whipped his head around and looked right at me. I smiled and asked this principal, "Do you pay your teachers extra for all of their work, above and beyond the contracted workday?"

He replies, "Why, no, we do not have the funding for that. If we could get more funding, we could pay them for it all!"

I look right at the governor and say, "Remember when I talked to you about parent involvement?" Then I looked at this principal and said, "In my day, parents volunteered in the school. Parents were there for breakfast with their children at home, parents helped in the lunchroom, parents came after school and helped the teachers and students, parents were there on the weekend to coach their kids' teams. Where are your students' parents? Why not encourage parent involvement and quit expecting your teachers to take on those responsibilities?"

I again looked at this principal and pointed my finger, saying, "I would hate to be a teacher in your school. I need time during school to plan, make copies, and do any number of the things expected of me during the day. I need my own private time at lunch to regroup. As well, MY children need their mother there for them at breakfast. MY children need me to be there after school to take them to their activities and help with their homework. MY children need me to be there on the weekends to help on their teams and enjoy our time together." Again, I state, "I would hate to be a teacher in your school, and you should be ashamed to work them to death like that."

See, when you beat someone to death using their emotions as the driving force, you will end up with someone who is resentful, unappreciated, and who eventually quits the job and moves on. This isn't about the children and how they feel. This is about keeping parents out of the classroom so schools and the government can more easily control these little darlings. We should be encouraging the parents to become more involved. We should be welcoming them as often as they want to be there with their own children. It's called investment. If we invest in helping the parents be with their children and involved with their children's education, parents will invest in them and take the giant burden off the teacher's shoulders. It is only then that teachers can return to basics and be allowed to teach content to make our children smarter and more successful. That is all we want for them, isn't it?

Wrestling Teacher Again

I am once again subbing for the wrestling teacher, but this time, it is a block day, so there are only two classes. He had called me in advance of this day. I arrive, and he is still in the classroom. Even though he and I had communicated about today's assignment, seeing him in person always makes things a bit awkward. The students were in the room and looking at both of us with great confusion. The teacher starts rattling off directions and says he hasn't had time to write anything down. I catch that there is an assembly but have no clue of when and where and he reminds me it is block day, so classes are two hours long.

Business Class, Lift Lab High School

Bi-Polar Education

Lift Lab is a class done completely on computers and con-

sists of students who have failed too many classes throughout the year. Many are juniors or seniors who don't have any
more time in their schedule to re-take more classes. My step-
son had to do this for two years, along with summer school
because he had failed too many classes since freshman year.
It is not free, and the student's lack of discipline is a money
drain on the parents. This class is before and after school as
they are busy taking their regular, on-grade classes. This is
a self-guided, online learning, and test-taking class, and they
must be completely silent or get kicked out.

The teacher/leader of the Lift Lab has ultimate control
over these kids. As they take tests and quizzes and complete
assignments, the teacher is the only one who can move them
along through the approval process. Being a Friday, many are
absent, but the students here seem to be working well. There
are always a few who simply do not care and continue to do
nothing, knowing they are going to fail again. All of these kids
have already taken whatever course they are doing now, in
the normal course of the school year, so this is a re-do. Most
of the kids are progressing and moving forward where they
didn't in regular classes. Is this a testimony for online or
automated learning? Are our kids better robots being force
fed info in the desire to get out of high school? Do they even
care what the info is, and do they retain any beyond the chapter test or final exam?

I have things I wonder about sometimes. When I was
going to college we were taught about intrinsic and extrinsic
learning. Of course, all parents want to know their children
are learning intrinsically; learning because they want to be

smarter, their curiosity was peaked, and they retained so much information. We had it drilled into our heads to learn how to engage the student. We must give the students a thirst for learning and the drive to want to learn more. We were taught to utilize small-group learning as a means to get kids to relate to one another and incorporate games to make kids forget they are learning, while learning. We were taught to not use prizes or other incentives because that will make their learning extrinsic, and they will be like trained clapping seals doing a trick for a prize.

Yet we were told to set goals so students could strive to achieve a gold star or privileges like extra recess or a pizza party. Wait, aren't those prizes or incentives? Did the Baby Boomer generation get goodies and prizes when they did their homework or got an answer correct in class? I believe we have sent so many mixed messages to our burgeoning teachers that they have become bi-polar, trying to reach every intelligence while making sure no one feels left out. We give them rewards for learning and discipline when they don't. We sit them at computers for independent test prep yet create small group activities. Kids don't know which way to turn as they progress from grade to grade, teacher to teacher, and school to school. Yikes, what are we doing to education? No wonder parents want to send their children to private or charter schools, which isn't even a safe haven anymore due to political pressure to conform. Some parents choose to homeschool, where in some states like Arizona, you can actually teach your children whatever curriculum you wish as long as they are retaining content. Kids in school today aren't being schooled for life but are becoming robots who do what they are told, in a timely fashion. However, this goes against the grain of what they're being told in the home that they act out at school or in life. They are conflicted, and I call that Bi-Polar Education.

High School, Business Class

I find it funny how a student's mind will go blank on process and procedure as soon as a sub walks in for the day. They act like they've never been in this classroom, and it isn't almost the end of the year. This is a three-day substitute job, and I've spoken personally to the teacher. She made it very clear that the students know exactly what info they need for the next three days to finish their year-end research paper. Most of these students are seniors, with a few juniors, and they are to write a real resume using creative license, along with a research paper about their future. This is a business class, so it seems appropriate.

The minute I walk in and start talking about them getting to work, they freak out. There are protests and hollerings about how they had no idea about this and have zero idea what to do or where to start. I explain to them that they have me for the next three days and I have spoken to their teacher, at length. They calm a bit, but very few of them know where to start or what to do.

There was a senior boy in the room who was very good natured and hangs next to his friend as they work in the computer lab. He's average height, with long sandy hair, blue eyes, and a scruffy beard. I see he's not doing any work, so I ask him if he's done already, and he says, "Oh! No, I'm not working today. See, I have a hockey game later." He smiles this huge, friendly smile and sits back like it is totally normal to make that choice. Good thing I'm not his normal teacher and just a sub. I would not be happy with that answer.

Observing behavior in an all-computer setting is always interesting. The teacher assigns an online research project, and kids are confused. They whine and fumble, and some start to play games or go on their email out of frustration. Do I help by giving them more info or let them figure it out and have it graded according to what they did? I prefer not to spoon-feed them because it creates a dependence on the teacher or adult, and they are less likely to search on their own. If they are forced to figure it out, they will generally strive higher. Process and procedure are necessary, but sometimes a little leeway can make the student thrive.

Very few of these students know what to do or where to start. I give instructions from what I assume is what is expected. The lesson plans say, "Students will write a research paper and write a resume." Nothing more. As an aside, I am always shocked when a teachers leaves such brief or non-existent lesson plans. What do they expect a sub to do, read their minds?

I write some links which I am aware of to help them, and some notice and start working. However, I believe most have never seen a real resume and do not understand what one is. They keep writing in their summary, "I am a junior in high school," "I am a good person."

These students worked with me for three days on this year-end project, which was due the day the teacher returned. Why in the world would a teacher have a sub work with kids on a major year-end project? I left a long note for the teacher explaining that only half of the students seemed to make the effort to get the assignments done as well as there being great confusion about one portion. I left my name and number, so if she had any questions, she could call me. We had computer availability issues along with some who were absent two of the three days.

The teacher never called me, and I wondered what became of the projects. Was it just busy work which she never intended to grade? The lack of respect between teacher and sub is frightening. These were juniors and seniors with only a week or two of school left. I cannot express how much of a gap there is in a child's education when a teacher is absent. If the teacher does not try to use a consistent sub or at least have communication with them, the students end up losing a day or few.

I'm sure you recall when I did the four-week-long sub job for the seventh-grade teacher who was having her first baby. On my last day, I left her a long note with my phone number and name so she and I could talk about the past month. As a first-year teacher, I could help her with some of the things I had implemented which the kids liked and were thriving on. When I walked out late that last day, she was in the parking lot. I walked right up to her thinking she would thank me or at least say hello and ask a few questions, but she did none of the above. I told her I left her a note and looked forward to her call so we could talk. She nodded at me and mumbled, "Thanks," as she walked away from me. She never called or contacted me. Never! I'd left the grade sheet as well as homework papers, which I had not had a chance to grade yet. For student consistency, I thought she would want to talk to me.

Nothing. Nothing.

Plight/Life of a sub: Bathrooms! Bathrooms! Who's got a bathroom?!

I know I've talked about this before, but it is a plight subs are plagued with. Where is it? How fast can I get there and back? If you need to go between classes, the halls are so clogged with kids who don't look where they're going, you can't get there fast enough. So many times I just go in the girls' room with the students, if I can find it. At least at one high school, the faculty bathrooms are marked but at another, nothing! I spend so much time wandering and searching.

Lunch? When? Where? How long do I have? A Lunch, B Lunch, C Lunch? Where is the lounge? Is there a microwave? Is there a fridge? People? Human life other than kids? Someone please talk to me! Heck, just look my way. The minute they look at you and realize they don't know you, they look away and run (not really run, but you know). Geez, I don't have leprosy! I've been subbing at the same high schools for many years and still have never met the principals or know where the lounges are.

Bell Schedule—Bong, bing, ring, zing overlapping bells, kids coming and going... How many minutes are the classes or passing periods? Some schools have obnoxious bells in different tones at different times of day. There's bell overlap for the various lunches and then bells for announcements. Bells, bells, bells all day! When do classes end? Then there's different schedules for different days. Certain days are block schedule at different schools and all are different. Some have special shortened periods all day, one day a week, so they can use the final hour for enrichment or remediation (kids who struggle, have missing assignments, or are failing). Fine! Please give a sub a heads up!

Where the heck am I going? I know I've written about this in other passages, but it has happened again and again. Certain high schools do not give the subs any information other than the teacher's schedule (with classroom numbers) and rosters for attendance. At least the other high school I sub at gives us a binder with maps and schedules. Apparently, they've built a new building and called it the "N" building. "N" is for New, I was told curtly by a security guard after I walked all the way around several hallways. Well, excuuuuuse me for living! As well, this new building is not attached and cannot be seen from any of the doors leading to the outside. I'm told I must walk out of the PE building, out past the dumpsters, behind the cafeteria, and Building N will be there. Hmmm, after ten minutes I finally found where I'm supposed to be for the next four hours. Where are the bathrooms? Don't get me started!

Changing the System

I make suggestions every time I sub, in order for a sub's life to be more simplified. They never take them or even ask me. I even leave my name and phone number for them to get my input, but I'm never called. For example, where are the bathrooms close to the classroom you are assigned to? On the map they provide (if it's provided), just make a red dot close to where they are and we can all relax. Wouldn't it be great to make a low-paying sub's life just a smidge easier and they will happily come back? Another thing is the markings of a building. At the local high school, they have several two-story buildings, and each one has a letter assigned to it. Nowhere on the outside of the building is a distinction of which building is which. The other day, after several years subbing here periodically, I was assigned room M223. M, M? The only information I could use was that it was on the second floor. I wandered around the different buildings for so long. I finally wandered into a building that had M in the room numbers, so I kept going. On the wall it said rooms 210–217 this way and rooms 201–209 that way. Where's room 223? I had to accost a woman as she was walking the hall and beg her to tell me where room 223 is. She pointed toward the "Room 210–217" sign. Ohhhkayy… It was the last room at the end of a T-shaped hall. Needless to say I was late to class and very frustrated. Simple sign markings would be immensely helpful, or even a detailed map in my sub folder. Seriously!

Student Observations

How do you get kids to stop taking pictures in class? I really don't care, but it is constant. Selfies, videos…how?

Senior Government class: This boy walks into class and announces that everyone can relax because he is here now. Yeah, as if anyone was waiting for him with bated breath. Not! He has a dynamic personality and hair to match. He is not irritating or abrasive in nature, so is basically harmless. He makes a big scene throwing away a wadded-up piece of paper, and after three attempts, he gives up and drops it in the can. A fellow student of his and I laugh at him and tell him maybe sports isn't his thing. He laughs as well, and we joke about how every team needs a water or ball boy. We all laugh and move on. At one point he sits in the rolling chair at the front of the room and says, "Is this what it's like to be a teacher?" I nod and tell him a big part of the job is making sure you all don't kill each other, and he and the other student agree. He pretends to be grading papers and looking up once in a while to point. He says, "This is easy." Oh, if he only knew. I guess he will know once he reads my book.

I must mention that as this is going on, another boy is shadow boxing in the back of the room. "Gotta practice for practice, you know." Funny!

In one class there was a kid who is the spitting image of Tom Cruise. He has heavy eyebrows, a big nose, deep-set eyes, stocky build, and about five-three, with brown spiky hair, a sleeveless sport shirt, and cargo shorts. It is his doppelganger!

Seems the fashion trend this year is leather hoodie jackets. They look like one is wearing a hoodie under a leather bomber jacket, but these are all one piece. Kind of cool!

High School Teachers Have No Humor

I feel the fun, humor, soul has been sucked out of them by the burgeoning adults they try to shove information into and have smacked their foreheads against that brick wall too many times. High school teachers are mocked, scoffed, sneered, and laughed at daily, all while trying to maintain a professional air and act above it all. No wonder that when I went to sit in the lunchroom to kill time, the teachers sit separately and don't smile or socialize. They want to be left alone. Many wear outdated clothing, old shoes (comfy and ugly), don't often do/wash their hair, make a small attempt at make-up, and drag around with an unaffected/afflicted look. I will walk around campus trying to catch their eyes and smile, but most pretend I do not exist. I know I'm a sub, but why treat me like a second-class citizen? On the other hand, I've met and experienced a few subs and they are boring, do-nothing dolts who let the kids run rampant. They pretend their brain is not functioning. Seriously? Be creative! Think! These are kids not monkeys. Talk to them, commiserate, read the handout with them. At least pretend to be interested!

My Son's Story of Having a Sub

My fourteen-year-old son told me a story about a sub he had for his art class. His art teacher was scheduled to be out for two days. He didn't say what the assignment was, but the sub was oblivious. His art teacher has supplies in buckets in the back of the classroom. While the sub was there, several students took the hot glue guns, plugged them in, and hot glued markers to the wall. This means they were out of their seats for quite a length of time. The students would have had to did they have to wait the five minutes for the gun to heat up, put in the slue sticks, grab a marker squirt hot glue on it, run to the wall, and wait for the glue to cool before they could leave it glued there; multiple times! What was the sub doing? Thinking? Were they sleeping, drugged, knocked out?!

The teacher came to her room that evening to check on things and found the disaster. She left a note for the sub to read to the class. The note asked for the students to remove and clean up the markers and not do that again. The students took the note and hot glued it to the wall as well. What goes through the mind of this alleged adult in charge? Does he/she see what's going on and thinks *Not my problem*? Are they saying, "Not my problem as long as they leave me alone"? Unbelievable! I guess this is one of the reasons which explain why teachers do not respect subs.

Seniors

Today I'm subbing in a senior-level History class. These are grown adult men who have facial hair and deep voices and women who are developing a sense of style and purpose. I remember being that age and feeling like school was just over. I felt I was ready to live my life, and why did I have to keep coming to this juvenile place and do what these boring adults wanted me to do? Some kids are working, some are sleeping, others are listening to music on their phones. Personally, I do not care what they do, as I am just the sub, and these are adults. They can make their own decisions on whether or not they want to do the work I have given them, which their teacher requires. May I also say I am flabbergasted that the teacher assigns book work about the Constitution and then has them watching a movie about the assassination of John F. Kennedy? I ask these kids if they know who was the vice president when Kennedy was shot, and they all say no. I ask them if they know the significance of why he was in Texas, and they say no. SAD! How do you get to be eighteen years old and not know the presidents? Okay, so I don't even know them all, but at least I know all about JFK and Lyndon B. Johnson. Schools these days should be all about learning how to read and write effectively, perform math skills (memorized times tables, division, fractions, percents), figure out how things work through science (not global warming crap), and the history of our country and other countries. NO religion, NO social issues, NO political rants, just how to work together and be an intelligent human being.

High School- Tenth-Grade English

Today is a block day and I do not have a break. Subs never know what, if any, breaks each teacher has. We are not told when we accept the job, and I try to come prepared. This does not always happen, but when the bathroom is right across that hall, I'm suddenly happy. This is my first sub job of this new school year, and I could not pass up an English class at this high school.

The first class of the day came in and they were great. I find this high school has quite a few strong personalities that can flourish here. Some personalities are stronger than others and some talk about sperm count. Let me describe this scene to you.

On block days, each class is two hours long. This is a special challenge because the teacher assigned the students to write all period. Some get right to it, but some are confused slow starters. As I circulate the room and help others, there are two boys who are not working at all but talking in low tones. I speak to them a few times, but they still won't get going. They aren't rude or disobedient but simply not doing the work assigned. As I circle back to them in the room, one of them holds up a can of Monster energy drink and asks, "Is it bad to drink one of these a day?" I answer yes and explain how it is bad for your liver. They agree and mention how a girl died of a heart attack from drinking too many. I nod and describe to them how these drinks cause liver and heart failure when consumed in large quantities.

One of the boys tells me it makes him pee a lot, and I say, of course, it is a diuretic. He is shocked and exclaims how he plays football and knows what that means. I nod and tell him that he needs to pay attention to what kinds of food and drink he puts into his body as he is a growing athlete and will pay for it later. We have a talk about the body's organs not working so well, and he mentions he is a diabetic and doesn't care. Then he says his sperm count is low and he wondered why. I try not to act shocked that we are now transitioning the conversation into sperm and say, "Well, if you don't feed your body properly, it will not perform as you wish." I told them I feed my husband and sons healthy greens so they have functioning organs, and leave it at that. They laugh as I walk away. Not the education I thought I'd be giving today but good, all the same. Like I have mentioned before, as a sub, the kids tell me everything because they think they will never see me again.

In the next period of the day, there is a boy who is flirty. You can tell he uses his looks and charm to get what he wants, but he's nice about it. He's Hispanic, in shape, and has dimples. As I walk by to talk to other students in his row, he tells me that I have pretty eyes. Oh boy. I nod and say thank you as I continue moving down the row. As I circle back, I see he is still not working and ask him if he needs help. He says he's okay, so I leave him alone, but when I circle back near his side of the room, he interrupts another student to talk to me. "You know, your eyes aren't really brown," he starts to tell me. I completely ignore him and know the game he's playing.

The interesting part of teaching/subbing is the challenging dance with students who are sometimes more mature in mind and body than the others. Some students are neither but have been exposed to adult themes at a young age and use their fellow students or teachers as prey. It is a teacher's job to never let the students get so comfortable that it opens the door for sexual innuendo to interfere.

When I taught sixth grade, the team was made up of myself, a pregnant woman about thirty years old, a married man in his mid-thirties, and a twenty-two-year-old ex-cheerleader first-year teacher. The younger teacher was extremely casual with the students. She allowed them to call her by her first name and allowed them stay in at lunch to have gossip sessions and chat about their relationships. She would tell them all about her life with her husband and how she wanted to have a baby. She wore tight pant or short miniskirts with low-cut tops and heels now and then. The boys would whistle at her, and she would laugh. The girls would look at her and wish to be like her while cattily dressing each other down. When I talk about exposing children to adult themes too early, I do not only mean movies and video games. I also mean influential adults who act immature and cause a child to think there is more of a personal relationship forming, instead of a professional teacher/student atmosphere. I spoke to her a few times about how she is too casual with the students, but she shooed me away and said I'm old school. She suggested I try her method, and I politely declined.

She always struggled getting the kids to do their homework and had quite low grades, which means the students were not performing for her, academically. She would give them second, third, and fourth chances to complete assignments or re-take quizzes or tests. She spent all of her time before and after school as well as lunch and prep time with the kids or talking to parents. When she had a few minutes before her room was filled with students at lunch, she would sit with us and whine about the problems she was having with the students. The three of us would nod and look at each other. She was very sure she was doing everything right and never took our advice. I again refer to the chapter where I talk about teacher professionalism and the nature of education today. There is a direct correlation to this and the state of our students' performance.

Anyone listening?

Crickets.

Many principals and superintendents think education needs more testing and test prep and that parents are test-score driven. This is the media narrative and is not the case. The more we test prep and test these kids yet do not provide a professional atmosphere, the poorer and poorer they perform.

Teacher With No Control

Science teacher who had zero control, always asked students to stop behavior and allowed them to argue (plea) their case.

I accept this subbing job, knowing that I am the teaching assistant for the day. I travel from classroom to classroom, helping teachers who have special ed students in the room. They are being mainstreamed, so they do not have to be isolated away from the general ed population, but they still require some assistance with their attention and learning style. I will not talk about the other classes as they were nothing out of the ordinary but will focus on this one class and teacher.

This class is freshman science, and the teacher is my age but in his first year. He is a new dad who seems extremely stressed out and frustrated. It is the eighth month of a nine-month school year, and he has been battling with this group of kids all year. As I sit in the back of the room, he begins to give directions for today's lesson, which is a packet of worksheets closely related to his lecture.

The students have had their way with this teacher for so many months, they can no longer listen to him or stop their juvenile behavior. Some are openly talking while he talks, getting out of their seats to walk over to a friend, whistling a tune, laughing, and making jokes. The teacher addresses each disruption personally, asking each student to "Please stop," or "Why are you doing this?" or "How come you will not listen?" or "Come on, guys, let's all work." The kids laugh at him and say things like, "We weren't talking," or "We weren't doing anything," or "You're crazy, teacher!" When he turns to walk away, they make faces and gestures. I cannot sit by and be silent any longer. I know how to deal with these kids, but I do not want to step on his toes. When I realize he has no toes to be stepped on, I get out of my seat.

We are a mere ten minutes into a two-hour class, and in light of the ensuing bedlam I start to swiftly walk toward one of the students who is the most aggressive. He and the group around him see me coming and smile. I lean in close and say,

"You WILL stop this childish behavior and listen to your teacher." I walk away while he blusters and comes up with plenty of excuses, but I neither turn around nor listen. The whole time, the teacher is continuing to give his lecture and direct the kids to the packet. I quietly walk to the next group who are out of their seats and put one finger on one boy's arm. I apply the smallest pressure, and he sinks to his seat, looking up at me. I lean in and tell him, "You WILL listen to the teacher and stay in your seat." He begins his blustering, but again, I do not listen and walk away. I go back to my seat in the corner and wait.

The room gets quieter, but the poor behavior continues. The teacher stops his lecture and starts to approach the student, but I intercept him by saying very loudly from across the room, "Stop right now. Sit!" and the boy sits. The teacher looks at me and goes back to the front of the room. Things progress like this for about ten minutes, and finally, the kids are starting to quiet and work, and the teacher is still talking. As the teacher is lecturing on and on, going through the many pages of this packet, the kids are asking questions. Some are lost because they weren't listening, and some simply cannot find the information in the book. I circulate the room, helping and making them feel successful. There are still a select few who insist on misbehaving, so I have to stay close and admonish those a few times. At some point I catch a boy with a racquet ball, and he keeps bouncing it on the floor. It rolls away at some point, and I get my hands on it. He begs me to give it back, and I say no, but I do so real close to his ear so other kids aren't distracted. He gets a little louder, and I tell him if he doesn't quiet down, I will never give him the ball. He gets quiet, but I hold on to the ball until the end of class. Lord help the teacher in his next class.

After class is over, all the kids file out, and the day is done; the teacher asks if I can stay behind and talk to him. Sure I can, and we begin chatting. He asks me if I could tell how poorly the students treat him? I say yes and can tell him why if he'd like. I tell him it won't make him happy but will help immensely. He tells me it is okay, that he is regretting becoming a teacher and needs help. He says he wishes I could be in the classroom with him every day. I laugh and tell him it is not possible, but here is what I suggest.

I tell him he is coddling them too much. He is not their friend and shouldn't speak casually to them until he knows they can be respectful. He is giving them packets which are ninety percent done, they just have to fill in a few blanks. Too easy and they don't have to put much effort in. I tell him when he asks a student to do something, say it in a commanding voice with no please or nice tone. Do not ask them questions, only give commands: "Sit down," "Pay attention," "Do not do that," Work," "Study"… and walk away. Do not wait for them to argue or whine. Give them your back and walk away. If they are misbehaving and you direct them, do it with authority and confidence. This whole "Come on, guys, please work" is weak, and the kids know it. If they whine or talk back to you, do not give them a second to know you hear them. I like to say, "You WILL study" or "You will sit quietly and read." It's like the power of suggestion and really works.

He blinks rapidly as I am telling him this and seems blown away. I ask him how old his child is, and he says, "Almost two." I ask him if he plans to give his child commands or let him talk back and whine. He stops and looks at me, then it seems the light comes on in his brain. He seems to make the connection to teaching and raising a child. Do you want him to be like that when he is in class? Do you want a teacher to get frustrated and want to quit teaching because of your child? He thanks me profusely and appreciates my honesty. I may have hurt his feelings, but it seems he was grateful. I am certainly no genius, and my children struggled as well, but I learned and changed and wish to help others through this book and when I sub.

Subbing at Junior High

Why does our system cater to parents more than the teacher? Why does the system allow parents to mistreat and make demands of teachers? This morning, before my subbing day began, one of the other eighth-grade teachers came into my classroom. She immediately introduced herself (which is extremely rare) and started talking about how subs usually aren't honest about how the children behaved in any given day and how it is hard for the teacher to follow up the next day with discipline. She was going on and on about, "as a teacher, we need to know because the kids shouldn't get away with treating a substitute, poorly." I agreed, but she continued describing situations in which the kids have to tell her how the kids were instead of the sub and then the subs do not come back. I decided to go ahead and let her know why I completely understood her and have had those experiences myself. I told her I used to be a teacher and now just sub. Her eyes got wide, and she said, "Well, then, you understand. Did you retire?" I tell her no, I simply quit the teaching profession.

This teacher explains to me that she has been teaching nineteen years and she truly does not want to do it anymore. After telling her one of my "why I quit teaching" stories, she gets tears in her eyes as she says she is tired, and it is only five weeks into a new school year. She asks me to look at her eyes and see just how tired she is. I know she doesn't mean sleepy tired but mental exhaustion tired. I explain to her how my final year of teaching was so persecuting and oppressive, I decided to quit. This information spurs her to tell me what is going on in her classroom, this year, that is so exhausting. She says, "You know how every year there is always one difficult parent or child? Well, we have one who has been difficult for every teacher who has had her child through the years, and this year, it's my turn."

The parent is dissatisfied with the speed at which papers are graded and grades are entered into the grade system. She has met with the principal to make sure her demands are being met. She wants every teacher to grade her child's work first and enter the grade into the system, immediately. While this may seem a reasonable request, it is not always possible. I'm sure that all parents feel this way, and teachers do the best they can with providing immediate feedback. Each middle school teacher has five or more classes, each day, with thirty or more students in each class. Doing the math, this is approximately 150 students, which means that each quiz, test, homework assignment, or project the teacher grades is multiplied by 150, each day. Many times, teachers will go over the homework or quizzes with the students during class, but sometimes, it takes a few days or a week to get those grades entered into the system. Refer back to previous chapters where I describe how in any given day teachers will have to answer emails, take phone calls, attend meetings, make copies, go to the bathroom, and plan for the days to come. As well, they must squeeze in time for grading papers and sitting at the computer to input those grades. A teacher gets ONE class period per day, called a prep period, in which they have time to take care of all the aforementioned tasks. Oftentimes, other teachers need to speak to them, or parents wish to come to the school to talk about their child, or the principal takes that free time to have a small meeting of the minds. In any case, the forty-five- to sixty-minute span of time every day is not enough to devote to only one student above and beyond all others and tasks. Most content-area teachers spend their nights, weekends, and holidays grading stacks of papers and sitting down to input grades, while most people who work a job, punch out, and go home. Teachers do not get to punch out and are always busy with the long and ever-growing list of tasks they must get done in any given day.

As well as the demand this parent is making on this teacher, they also send lengthy emails, berating said teacher for not putting their child first. This parent also wants stats for the classroom for every test and homework assignment, like class averages and patterns of behavior. The parent shares everything with the student and said student comes to school talking to the other kids about how, "My mom and our teacher are having communication problems." The teacher has been told by the principal to comply and not let it bother her. As told in previous chapters, this is impossible and always turns into a problem. The administration needs to have a serious talk with this parent about proper communication with a teacher and help them understand that their request is not always going to be possible. For this teacher and school's sake, I hope the support is there. This teacher surely wishes she could do anything but teach, and that is sad.

Sticky Note Plans

I had the opportunity to sub in a nineth- and tenth-grade English class. The teacher is the cheerleading coach and is on a trip with her squad. I was asked to take on three consecutive days for her and gladly accepted. I do not know her at all, but English is a breeze for me. However, her sub plans were a series of sticky notes on some printed out PowerPoint sheets. There was no schedule, order of tasks, who to contact for help or directions for where to find said PowerPoints to show to the students. Just a sticky note saying, "Show these to the class." Turns out it was in her Google docs file, which is online and uses her passwords. I have none of the above access so had to wing it. The students were wild while I was trying to navigate the sticky notes and hunt for papers and worksheets. This is immensely frustrating and is a perfect recipe for chaos. Nothing is worse than kids who have nothing to do and no clear direction. I truly wanted to walk out of class that day and never come back.

As well, I had a kid in that first class who is mildly mentally challenged and kept blurting out random words and hitting kids. While I was trying to figure out what to do with the students, he got out of his seat, ran to the front of the class, and shook his butt up and down at the other students. He laughed and laughed, and I had to yell at him to stop and sit down. I sure didn't like that, but what else was I to do? The classroom was falling apart, all because the teacher had not left clear direction. I had to stop what I was doing and scold him many times until his one-on-one aide finally came to the room and sat in the corner. She proceeded to do nothing to help or discipline him, and it fell on me again. To think, that was just ONE of FIVE classes. It also turned out that three of her classes were in one room, and her other classes were in the room next door. That was not stated on the plans, and it was a surprise to me when another teacher came in to use the room, shoving me out the door. I had to ask her where I was to go, and she pointed to the room next door. This meant I needed to gather ALL of my things and travel to the next room. When I got to the room next door, it was full of students who were talking, laughing, and moving about the room. Time to start all over with a new batch of students and begin trying to figure out what they were supposed to be doing. I was able to convince this other teacher to log in and find the Powerpoint for me to show, but that only worked on the first day with one class. It was back to square one on days two and three.

At the end of the third day, I wrote her a long note telling her exactly what went on and how frustrating it was. I let her know that I was a teacher for many years and have written many substitute plans. I wrote to her that she needs to be clear with her plans for the students, and a sub is someone who has zero idea what she is thinking, had been doing, or understands her filing system. I hoped next time she has to have a sub, she takes a better approach with clearer direction. I know it is not cool to dress down a teacher when I am but a lowly sub, but it must be done. If anyone can rip off the bandage of truth, I guess it shall be me.

These are the days that try a substitute's will to go on and care.

Conclusion

Many will ask themselves why a teacher becomes a teacher and then why would they get disgruntled or possibly leave? Making the tough decision to leave teaching altogether was not all my own but for the sake of my sanity and health. I absolutely loved the students, both difficult and easy, but it was not enough to make me stay. My last year as a substitute teacher was challenging, and I fiercely miss those students whom I saw on an intermittent basis.

My last day of substitute teaching in the same district and schools where I had been subbing for the past six years was the worst day I have ever had. The students were wonderful, but it was the adults who made it untenable. I was a para-professional aide for the classroom teachers, and my job was to assist with the severely disabled high school students as they learned content and traveled between classes and at lunch. I saw students who were blind, mentally disabled, had Down's Syndrome, were in a wheelchair due to Cerebral Palsy, were completely deaf, or had physical limitations and needed major assistance. I was the only aide with several different classroom teachers and about sixteen students.

I was treated like I was a pain in the behind to the classroom teacher because I asked too many questions, and they were on their phones or had to step out of the room to go grab food or a drink. I was yelled at by other aides in the PE class, scorned by other teachers in the lunchroom, and told I was stupid when I did not know to open milk for some students but not for others.

I witnessed aides and teachers pushing students, yelling at students, or ignoring them completely when they begged for help. I alerted admin, and they called me an interloper and to mind my own business. Why stay? Why subject myself to this abuse?

Thus ended my career as a teacher and subsequent substitute while I went back home to contemplate my future profession choices. I missed it terribly but did not feel I had a home anywhere in education. Reader, I want you to know my educational journey did not end there and I delight in writing my follow-up book. Stay tuned, and thank you for reading a snapshot of my experiences as a teacher and substitute.